THE NISGA'A TREATY

To Daniel
With sincere appreciation for
your contributions to my research
for this book.

Rick

THE NISGA'A TREATY

POLLING DYNAMICS AND POLITICAL COMMUNICATION IN COMPARATIVE CONTEXT

J. RICK PONTING

broadview press

Library and Archives Canada Cataloguing in Publication

Ponting, J. Rick
The Nisga'a treaty : polling dynamics and political communication in comparative context / J. Rick Ponting.

Includes bibliographical references and index.
ISBN 1-55111-790-8

1. Canada. Treaties, etc. 1999 May 4—Public opinion.   2. Nisga'a Indians—British Columbia—Claims—Public opinion.   3. Nisga'a Indians—Land tenure—British Columbia—Public opinion.   4. Indian land transfers—British Columbia—Public opinion.   5. Nisga'a Indians—British Columbia—Treaties—Public opinion.   6. Public opinion— British Columbia.   7. Government advertising—British Columbia.   8. Australian aborigines—Public opinion.   9. Public opinion—Australia.   10. Public opinion polls— Case studies. I. Title.

JL429.5.P64P65 2006   346.71104'320899741   C2006-902340-9

Broadview Press is an independent, international publishing house, incorporated in 1985. Broadview believes in shared ownership, both with its employees and with the general public; since the year 2000 Broadview shares have traded publicly on the Toronto Venture Exchange under the symbol BDP.
    We welcome any comments and suggestions regarding any aspect of our publications — please feel free to contact us at the addresses below, or at broadview@broadviewpress.com / www.broadviewpress.com

North America	UK, Ireland, and	Australia and
PO Box 1243,	Continental Europe	New Zealand
Peterborough, Ontario,	NBN International	UNIREPS
Canada K9J 7H5	Estover Road	University of
Tel: (705) 743-8990	Plymouth PL6 7PY	New South Wales
Fax: (705) 743-8353	United Kingdom	Sydney, NSW, 2052
customerservice	Tel: +44 (0) 1752 202300	Tel: + 61 2 96640999
@broadviewpress.com	Fax: +44 (0) 1752 202330	Fax: + 61 2 96645420
	enquiries@nbninternational.com	info.press@unsw.edu.au

PO Box 1015
3576 California Road,
Orchard Park, New York
USA 14127

Cover design and typeset by Zack Taylor, www.zacktaylor.com

Broadview Press Ltd. gratefully acknowledges the financial support of the Government of Canada through the Book Publishing Industry Development Program for our publishing activities.

This book is dedicated to the Nisga'a people, whose patience and perseverance in their quest for justice should not have been necessary, and to the Indigenous peoples of Australia, who are still waiting.

Contents

Acknowledgements

I wish to express my gratitude for the contributions of the many individuals who made this book possible. First and foremost are the interviewees, all of whom gave very generously of their time. Most were very accommodating and several invited me into their home. A debt of gratitude is also owed to BC government information officer Carly Hyman, whose dedication in replying to my Freedom of Information requests under very difficult retrieval conditions resulted in the transfer to me of valuable data on Nisga'a Treaty advertising requisitions, contracts, and content. I am also indebted to Professor Enrico L. Quarantelli, who not only introduced me to the Blumerian perspective on public opinion polling that is the foundation of a large part of the research reported here, but also served as an inspiring role model for me as a professional sociologist. I am grateful also to University of Calgary Vice-President (Academic) Professor Ronald Bond, whose office helped fund the research and who was a visionary ally of aboriginal priorities at the University. Finally, I wish to express my appreciation to Michael Harrison and Greg Yantz, and their colleagues at Broadview Press for their support, understanding, facilitation, and professionalism throughout the process of bringing this project to fruition.

Foreword

Purposes

This book focuses on the adoption of the Nisga'a Treaty and the work of Australia's Council for Aboriginal Reconciliation. The book has two main purposes, the first of which is to advance our understanding of these historically important, contemporary efforts to realign relations between Indigenous peoples and the larger society. The Nisga'a Treaty case study necessarily takes us into a consideration of what, in more generic terms, might be called the marketing stage of the policy process. In pursuing this first purpose, the book is essentially a political ethnography that takes the reader "backstage" with the key political actors involved. Conceptual jargon is kept to a minimum so as to make the message accessible to as wide an audience as possible. A second main purpose is to contribute to our understanding of the dynamics of public opinion polling (and to a lesser extent, focus groups) in all its phases, from before the birth of a poll through to its use by political decision makers.

The methodological inspiration for the research comes from renowned sociologist Hubert Blumer. In a long-neglected portion of his much-discussed[1] presidential address to the American Sociological Association, Blumer (1948) advocated a new approach to the study of public opinion. Said he,

> a model should be constructed, if it can be at all, by working backwards instead of by working forward. That is, we ought to begin with those who have to act on public opinion and move backwards along the lines of the various expressions of public opinion that come to their attention, tracing these expressions backward through their own various channels. (p. 549)

Such an approach views the public opinion that gets registered with decision makers as a social construct, a product of social interactions and interpretations.

---

1. For some of that discussion, see Converse (1987, pp. S13–16) in the special 1987 supplement of *Public Opinion Quarterly* that celebrated 50 years of public opinion polling scholarship in America. Referring to Blumer's critique of quantitative polling research, the editor of that issue, Eleanor Singer, went so far as to begin her "Editor's Introduction" (1987, p. S1) with the bold sentence "Blumer was wrong." She characterized (p. S1) that issue of the journal as celebrating "the triumph of the quantitative." Miller (1995, p. 111) is one of the few to explicitly address Blumer's very specific call for a new public opinion research strategy that works backwards from the decision makers who use polling data. Salmon and Glasser (1995, p. 443) argue "Blumer's critique of public opinion polling is as timely today as it was in 1947.... In many ways, Blumer's critique is of greater significance today."

However, academic research in the spirit of this call by Blumer has been sparse. Heith's (1998) account of polling in the Nixon, Ford, Carter, and Reagan White Houses and Jacobs's and Shapiro's (1995/96) account of Nixon's calculated manipulation of (and interference with) national pollsters are two of the few analyses to be found in a Blumerian vein. The present book seeks to contribute toward a more widespread recognition of the Blumerian "constructivist" approach to the study of public opinion.

In the interests of manageability, Blumer's backwards tracing is pursued here primarily to the point of the production and interpretation of public opinion data. The deployment of the thus-interpreted data to shape government behaviour (advertising) also receives detailed attention, but that is more in the service of my first purpose than my second.

Contextually, the book is situated within the debate on the essence of democratic politics and leadership (e.g., Jacobs & Shapiro, 2000; Lippman, 1925). In particular, the book is highly relevant to the issue of whether government is (or should be) responsive to public opinion and the issue of whether it is appropriate in a democracy for government to be "proactive" (some would say "manipulative" while others would say "educative") in seeking to lead and shape that public opinion. While the British Columbia case study clearly reveals a highly proactive government using polling to shape the public discourse and opinion on the Nisga'a Treaty, it is not my intention to take up that debate.

Caveats

Certain caveats are in order. First, the descriptive mandate of the book is a relatively narrow one. By no means does the book purport to offer the full story of the Australian undertaking at national reconciliation or the British Columbia government's implementation of the Nisga'a Treaty. *It is important to emphasize that in our main case study, the Nisga'a Treaty, the polling and communications functions were only part of the work of the much larger Nisga'a Treaty Implementation Project team.* Other work of that implementation team included such activities as drafting the legislation and preparing ministries for their responsibilities when the Treaty came into effect. The polling and advertising were part of a tightly co-ordinated whole overseen by Deputy Minister to the Premier, Doug McArthur. Furthermore, even my account of the selling of the Treaty is a partial one. For instance, nothing is included on the selling of the Treaty by Nisga'a leaders to the Nisga'a people, non-Native politicians, and others. Virtually nothing is included on the federal government's efforts to sell the Treaty, such as in Parliament where it encountered vociferous opposition from the then Reform Party. Nor is there any examination here of the British Columbia Opposition's efforts to sell its definition of the situation to British Columbians in an attempt to scuttle the Treaty. Instead, insofar as the Nisga'a Treaty is concerned, the focus of the present volume is primarily on the British Columbia government's public opinion polling and on the advertising and public information campaign that accompanied that polling.

Within that focus, attention is further concentrated on the period from summer 1998, when the Treaty was signed, to the end of 1998, when the period of intense polling and advertising ended.

A second caveat is that the Nisga'a Treaty polling situation was highly atypical compared to most government (as opposed to political party) polling. In particular, the Nisga'a Treaty was the highest political priority of the government and control over polling about it was highly centralized in the Office of the Premier. The polling and advertising were also funded at extraordinarily generous levels.

Thirdly, it is important to remember that the British Columbia polling that is a major focus of this book was only one of the provincial government's inputs on the contours of public opinion on the Treaty. Additional sources of input on public opinion included, among other things, the approximately four hundred "town hall" meetings held to discuss the Treaty, the media (including letters to the editor) monitoring done by the implementation team, audience reaction to the numerous speeches made by the Premier and the Minister, and constituents' input passed along by NDP Members of the Legislative Assembly (MLAs).

A final caveat is that the Australian case study included in this volume is mainly intended to complement the BC case study and to broaden the basis from which generalizations are drawn. No attempt is made to give a full account of the full scope of the public opinion research done by the Council for Aboriginal Reconciliation over its ten year existence.

Canadian Public Opinion on Aboriginal Issues

Even though the specifics of public opinion polling results are not a major focus of this volume and consideration of those results is largely confined to Chapter Six and a small portion of Chapter Eight, some words of context about public opinion on aboriginal issues in Canada are in order here. On the basis of my own national surveys in 1976 (with Roger Gibbins) and 1986, and my analysis of other national survey data sets (e.g., 1979, 1998) that have been given to me, I can make several generalizations.[2] First, Canadians have little knowledge and awareness of aboriginal issues. Secondly, Canadians tend to be supportive of aboriginal leaders' positions on aboriginal issues, although not of positions that seem to violate strongly held values of equality. "Militant" tactics also garner very little support. Regional variations are pronounced, as British Columbians generally exhibit more knowledge of aboriginal issues than other Canadians, but slightly less sympathy. On land claims issues, British Columbians are markedly less sympathetic to aboriginal positions than the Canadian average. Finally, non-Native public opinion on aboriginal issues tends to be rather inchoate.

---

2. See Ponting (1988a, 1988b, 2000a).

Chapter One: Introduction

Importance

The vigorously contested Nisga'a Treaty was a matter of vital importance to First Nations, to the then Premier and his New Democratic Party government, and to other British Columbians. Its importance stemmed, in part, from the fact that it was the first treaty to be successfully negotiated in the province in the modern era and, as such, in many quarters was viewed (at least initially) as a policy template for the fifty other treaties to be negotiated in its wake. Its importance also derived from the severely beleaguered government's belief in the moral rectitude of its position and the resultant determination to see it implemented. Furthermore, the government saw the Nisga'a Treaty as a "wedge issue" by which it could differentiate itself from the Liberal opposition. No issue had higher priority for the government during Fall 1998. Finally, the Treaty took on added importance when its opponents raised the political stakes not only through a discourse that went well beyond the usual polarization of British Columbia politics, but also through earnest attempts (e.g., a constitutional challenge) to block its implementation. The outcome of the political struggle would be laden with historical significance, regardless of who won.

In this highly charged political context, the ratification of the Treaty became contested terrain. Interest in who was winning the contest for public opinion was intense, and deployment of resources was substantial. For instance, the provincial government mounted a multi-million dollar advertising campaign, including a quarter million dollar public opinion polling project. A major purpose of this volume as political ethnography is to tell the story of that public opinion polling and advertising project, particularly how it was handled inside the government of the day.

Premises and Processing

This historical research is guided by certain premises loosely derived from symbolic interactionist theory, particularly from its social constructionist offshoot (Blumer, 1969; Holstein & Miller, 2003; Spector & Kitsuse, 1977) and applied here to public opinion polling. The first premise is that there is nothing automatic about the registering of public opinion with decision makers. Public opinion findings are not just a product (a report) handed to decision makers. Rather, the registering of public opinion with decision makers is a *social process* influenced by social and political factors such as trust, confidence, and norms of professionalism, among others. Furthermore, decision makers are not necessarily aloof bystanders; rather, they sometimes are intimately involved in influencing or even controlling the work of moulding and gathering public opinion, as Jacobs and Shapiro (1995/96) so vividly documented in the case of the Nixon White House. Thus, the processes involved in deciding to conduct a poll or focus group, funding it, constructing the questionnaire and gathering the data, analysing the data, interpreting the data, and disseminating those interpretations and data must be understood. Finally, it is assumed that *meaning and significance inhere in potentially every stage* of the process, such as choice of data collection firm; sampling of respondents; sampling of the universe of potential questions; phrasing of the questions; analytic methods chosen and foregone; and attribution of meaning and significance to the results, especially in communications with the decision maker(s). Any of these parts of the process is worthy of attention. The same can be said about each part of the public opinion *shaping* phenomenon (e.g., message framing, choice of advertising agency, choice of media).

So, what is meant by the term "processing of public opinion data"? The reference is to the dynamics of precisely those processes listed above—from the decision to conduct a poll to the registering of interpreted results with decision makers and others. This conveniently skirts the much-debated question of what is public opinion, and it favours a definition of public opinion as that which comes to be registered with decision makers. This approach recognizes, though, that that which comes to be registered with decision makers is problematic—very much a social construction.

The main focus of the narrative will be the case study of the British Columbia government's processing of public opinion on the Nisga'a Treaty in the summer and autumn of 1998. However, that research is part of a larger project involving the Government of Australia's processing of public opinion on the issue of the reconciliation process between Australian Indigenous people and the larger Australian society. The research also encompassed the Government of Canada's processing of public opinion on the Nisga'a Treaty and on the issue of an apology to aboriginal people in Canada. Chapter Eight presents a case study sketch of the Australian events, while Chapter Nine makes some generalizations based on the case studies.

Limits of Generalizability

It would be potentially dangerous to generalize too broadly from any case study, for as one interviewee said in reference to the British Columbia polling and advertising campaign, and the centralization of that in an inner circle with a passionately engaged elite, "I've never seen anything even remotely like it in the [many] years I've been [here]" (Interviewee #14291). Hence, generalizations or hypotheses derived from the Nisga'a case study should possibly be restricted to issues that take on paramount importance in the jurisdiction involved. Even then, the utmost caution is warranted, for in important respects this case study falls at or near one extreme of a continuum of politicization and of procedure. Although the propositions advanced in Chapter Nine are couched in fairly sweeping terms, we

---

BOX 1.1
A Statistical Glimpse of the Nisga'a Population Living on Nisga'a Lands

The 2001–02 Aboriginal Peoples Survey (APS) conducted by Statistics Canada in conjunction with the 2001 Census provides socio-demographic-economic information about the Nisga'a people living on Nisga'a Lands. The APS reported a population there of 1,660 persons, of whom about 30% are under age 15. Under the Treaty, we can expect the population on Nisga'a lands to increase due to in-migration of Nisga'a members as opportunity structures expand in the four communities.

Compared to many southern Canadian First Nations, the Nisga'a have preserved their language well, as 84% of Nisga'a adults (aged 15 and over) report being able to speak or understand an aboriginal language, including 60% who understand their primary aboriginal language "very well" or "relatively well" and 43% who speak it "very well" or "relatively well." Twenty per cent use their primary aboriginal language at home all or most of the time. Among the children under age 15, 78% speak or understand an aboriginal language, but only 23% can speak an aboriginal language "very well" or "relatively well."

The residential school experience was a common one among the Nisga'a and their extended families; 22% of the adults in the four communities reported having attended a residential school and 97% said that they had family members who attended.

The unemployment rate in 2000 was 38%. Many members of the four communities engaged in the traditional economic activities of hunting, fishing, or gathering. For instance, almost half (44%) of the adults fished for food. (The Nass is one of the most important salmon rivers in British Columbia.) Over half (57%) of adults used a computer in the twelve months before the study, and 44% used the Internet.

Source: Statistics Canada. (2001). *Aboriginal Peoples Survey Community Profiles*. Retrieved August 27, 2004, from <http://www12.statcan.ca/english/profil01aps/home.cfm>.

---

must always bear in mind that those generalizations were grounded in cases that, in important respects, were atypical.

Context

The Nisga'a People and BC Land Claims Policy

The Nisga'a are an aboriginal people whose traditional territory is centred on the Nass River Valley in northwestern British Columbia. At the time of the signing of the Treaty, they numbered around 5,500 persons. Most Nisga'a members live in four communities (New Aiyansh, Gitwinksihlkw, Laxgalts'ap, and Gingolx) along the river in the traditional territory or in Vancouver, Terrace, or Prince Rupert. Members belong to one of four tribes or Pdeek: Eagle, Killerwhale, Ravena, and Wolf. Under the Treaty, the Nisga'a nation-level (as opposed to community-level) government is called the Nisga'a Lisims Government and is located in New Aiyansh, about 100 kilometres by road from Terrace.

The Nisga'a stand out as being among the best organized, most politically experienced and sophisticated, and most determined aboriginal people in British

Columbia or Canada.[1] The Nisga'a were leaders in the early twentieth-century land claims movement in British Columbia (Woolford, 2005, p. 74–75). From at least the 1960s onward, their leaders held a particularly high political profile. Furthermore, the Nisga'a land claim, which dated back to a Nisga'a petition in 1887, came to dominate the provincial policy agenda on aboriginal rights. Pursuant to their "moral victory"[2] in the Supreme Court of Canada in the famous Calder case, in 1996 the Nisga'a entered negotiations with the federal government on a so-called "comprehensive claim." These negotiations were separate from the BC Treaty Commission process.[3]

Eventually, on August 9, 1990, over one hundred years after the original Nisga'a claim, Social Credit Premier Bill Vander Zalm reversed British Columbia's earlier policy of refusing to negotiate aboriginal land claims. That opened the door to the eventual settlement of the longstanding Nisga'a grievance, for the provincial government now joined the negotiating table with the Nisga'a and the federal government. The Nisga'a Agreement-in-Principle (AIP), involving the Nisga'a and the provincial and federal governments, was announced on February 15, 1996, three days before Glen Clark won the NDP leadership campaign and shortly before the provincial election had to be called.[4] Some fifty other claims were in submission or in one or another stage of negotiation when, on August 4, 1998, amidst great ceremony and political theatre,[5] the Nisga'a Treaty was signed by Nisga'a leaders and the federal and provincial governments.

The Paradox of Polling Data: Allure and Scepticism

Public opinion data can be put to many uses. Broadly speaking, public opinion data are collected by governments for one or more of the following purposes: to reduce political uncertainty, to increase the autonomy of state actors vis-à-vis the mass public or other governments or government departments, to identify the bounds of the possible, and to aid in the justification or legitimation of state policy that is under consideration or has been formulated already. Accordingly, polling data have a powerful allure for many politicians and for those public servants who, by virtue of their position at the senior levels of the government bureaucracy, have come to

---

1. For more on the long journey of the Nisga'a people toward justice, see Molloy (2000).

2. The Supreme Court justices were evenly split, and the deciding vote was cast against the Nisga'a on the basis of a technicality, namely, that they had not obtained the permission of the Crown to sue the Crown. However, the fact that a body of his intellectual peers attributed legitimacy to the Nisga'a claim led Prime Minister Pierre Trudeau to reverse his policy and recognize the existence of aboriginal rights. As part of that policy reversal, he introduced the Comprehensive Claims policy under which the Nisga'a treaty was eventually negotiated.

3. For a discussion and critique of that larger BC treaty negotiations process, see Woolford (2005).

4. The NDP, under leader Mike Harcourt, was elected on October 7, 1991. Thus, February of 1996 was very late in the party's mandate.

5. The political theatre continued with the ceremonies surrounding the opening of debate on the Treaty in the BC legislature. See Beatty (1998c).

be known in the literature as "political administrators" (Heclo & Wildavsky, 1974; see also Box 1.2). Their attraction to public opinion data has been described by participants in this project in terms of drug addiction. Said one regular attendee at cabinet meetings, "They're a bit seduced by it.... Polling is like the crack cocaine of politicians.... Ordinarily, you could hear a pin drop in Cabinet when somebody says we're going to do a poll." Said the BC Premier's Deputy Minister, "Polling is like a drug—the more you do it, the more you want it. It's intriguing and interesting ... [but] you have to be careful not to become captured by public opinion. Use it carefully and don't become dependent upon it."

Notwithstanding the allure of polling data, it is, of course, not decision makers' only source of information on public opinion, and it is not necessarily held in uniformly high regard. Pétry and Mendelsohn's (2004) study found that only a slight majority (56%) of 120 Canadian federal policy actors[6] regarded polls conducted by the government as "very important" indicators of "what the public thinks." Even focus groups (at 60%), newspaper articles (73%) and polls conducted outside government and made public through the media (76%) scored higher as indicators of what the public thinks. Pétry and Mendelsohn also found that half of their respondents agreed (43% strongly) with the statement "Public opinion is easily manipulated by the media, politicians, and spin doctors." Fuchs and Pfetsch (1996, p. 20) found that a large majority of government actors in public information agencies do use other contacts with citizens as a mechanism for monitoring public opinion. Herbst (1998) reports similar findings from her Illinois study. Similarly, as noted in the Foreword, in the Nisga'a case, polling and focus groups were merely two among many inputs to government on how the AIP (and later the Treaty) was being received. Formal advisory bodies—both sector-specific (e.g., forestry, mining, governance) and a province-wide Treaty Negotiations Advisory Committee comprising some thirty organizations (e.g., labour, environmental, and business organizations)—were used to aggregate and articulate some such input. Cabinet members and members of the Legislative Assembly provided further input, as did the hundreds of outreach meetings (e.g., "town hall" sessions) held around the province.

In fact, two highly placed individuals involved in the Nisga'a project expressed scepticism toward polling. One (#14291) went so far as to say,

> You don't need a poll to know what's going on out there. It's quite
> easy if you listen to people and if you get out very much.... Most
> polling is just unbelievably bad—a lot of money we spend just to
> tell us what we already know.... I think the Nisga'a case was one of
> the rare ones where we got some useful advice.... Maybe the lesson
> for government [from the Nisga'a campaign] is that you have to do

---

6. Their respondents included cabinet ministers and other government and opposition members of Parliament, party officials, executive assistants, deputy ministers, associate deputy ministers, and pollsters.

that kind of extensive amount of polling to really be useful, as opposed to these "snapshots" that just tell you what you already know.

Despite that scepticism, most in the inner circle—including the Premier—were intimately involved with the polling for the advertising campaign.

The Inner Circle and Other Actors on the Nisga'a Project

The term "inner circle" is used here to refer to those who were most influential in the *design and strategic decision making* of the polling, advertising, and public information campaigns on the Nisga'a project. Most members of the inner circle met daily as "the senior management team," although one member of the inner circle—namely Premier Clark—did not attend those daily morning meetings. To further complicate matters, some persons—whom we might call "key associates"—did attend those morning meetings with the senior management team and did play important roles, but are excluded from my definition of the inner circle because their degree of influence on matters of design and strategy was significantly less than that of the persons who are included. A third type of participant might be called the "supporting cast." Their roles were also vital to the success of the project. For instance, the widely respected former chief negotiator, Jack Ebbels, who is classified as among the supporting cast, sat at the Premier's side as expert advisor during some of the debate in the legislature.

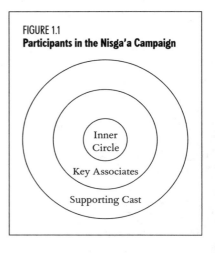

FIGURE 1.1
Participants in the Nisga'a Campaign

Inner Circle

Key Associates

Supporting Cast

With the above distinction in mind, we can diagram the participants in the polling, advertising, and public information campaigns on the Nisga'a Treaty as shown in Figure 1.1.

The "inner circle" comprised
- Glen Clark, Premier
- Doug McArthur, Deputy Minister to the Premier
- Shawn Thomas, advertising team leader
- John Heaney, assistant director of the project

Among the "key associates" were
- Ian Reid, polling expert (in inner circle for polling)
- Daniel Savas, vice-president of polling firm Angus Reid
- Don Zadravec, media relations team leader

- Clay Suddaby, Zadravec's successor
- Peter Lanyon, creative director of TV advertising
- Mike Krafczyk, of Copeland Communications, who was responsible for print advertising
- Tim Pearson, who led the writing team
- others such as other writers and the caucus liaison person

The "supporting cast" included such people as
- Dale Lovick, Minister of Aboriginal Affairs
- NDP MLAs, such as Dan Miller from the Terrace area
- Jack Ebbels,[7] Deputy Minister (DM) of Aboriginal Affairs and former chief provincial negotiator on the Nisga'a file
- Peter Smith, Ministry of Aboriginal Affairs (MAA) communications director
- Phillip Steenkamp, Ebbels's successor as DM
- Chuck Phillips, Peter Lanyon's partner in the Lanyon-Phillips advertising agency
- Nikki McCallum, Thomas's assistant
- the media monitors
- MAA personnel who staffed the toll-free telephone lines
- outreach workers who participated in community meetings
- the logistics supervisor for the project
- others

The lines between the sectors sometimes became blurry, and a given individual might be in one sector at one point in the project but move to another sector at another point in the project when his or her skills and expertise were less needed or more needed. For instance, a case could be made for Mike Krafczyk as a member of the supporting cast at some points in the campaign and also for Don Zadravec as a member of the inner circle at certain times during the campaign.

One might anticipate that the office of the provincial Minister of Aboriginal Affairs would be a key player in the polling and advertising decisions on the Nisga'a issue. However, that was not the case, in part because Dale Lovick had been appointed to the portfolio only a few months earlier, in February 1998. Although he and the Premier were "front and centre" during the debates in the

---

7. Jack Ebbels attended the morning meetings of the inner circle only about once per week, by his recollection. He is listed here as a member of the supporting cast, due to the way in which his expertise was used by the team. He told me, "They'd ask my views on tactics, strategy, whatever they were up to, not on advertising strategy. I wasn't a supporter of what they were doing, and they knew it. It was a lot of money, and I thought the Treaty could sell itself, and it was a matter of simply putting out information about the Treaty. My chief role was in public communications—an awful lot of mass media interviews and in public meetings in communities all around BC to answer questions and tell what was in the Treaty…. My expertise was knowledge of the interest groups in BC on the ground, and [of] the Treaty."

legislature, the hallmark of the provincial polling and advertising campaign on Nisga'a was the fact that *decisions about it reflected the prevailing power structure in the government*. In particular, decision making on polling was highly centralized in the persons of the Premier and his Deputy Minister, Doug McArthur, while decision making on advertising was concentrated with McArthur and Shawn Thomas, both trusted appointees close to the Premier.

Glen Clark was a former labour organizer who entered electoral politics in his mid-twenties. He rose quickly to prominence in the Mike Harcourt NDP government and became Finance Minister in his early thirties. Demoted by Harcourt, allegedly for being too ideological, he was able to exact a cabinet appointment to an economic development portfolio known as Employment and Investment. A masterful campaigner, he won the NDP leadership when Harcourt stepped down. Like many other provincial premiers in Canada, he centralized much power in the Office of the Premier. Even some cabinet colleagues reportedly felt intimidated by him before his own personal political fortunes waned with the RCMP raid on his home on March 2, 1999. The Premier came to feel passionately about the Nisga'a Treaty issue and therefore attached an extremely high priority to the file. For about four months, it reportedly was a major preoccupation of his although, as noted, he did not attend the meetings of the senior management of the Nisga'a Treaty Implementation Project (NTIP) team, as it was called.

Deputy Minister Doug McArthur served in a role equivalent to that of campaign manager in an election campaign. Where trust and confidence were of vital importance, he obviously enjoyed the full and absolute trust and confidence of the Premier. After being designated to replace John Heaney, McArthur was fully in charge, even to the point of being the gatekeeper who selected what information would go to the NDP MLAs. McArthur was a seasoned professional with impeccable credentials. A Rhodes Scholar, former academic, and NDP cabinet minister (1978–82) in the Blakeney government in Saskatchewan, he was also well experienced in land claims and other aboriginal issues inside and outside British Columbia. For instance, he was Chief Land Claims Negotiator in Yukon, served as Deputy Minister of Aboriginal Affairs in BC, set up the new Nisga'a negotiating team in 1992, and served as a consultant to different aboriginal organizations. As Deputy Minister of the Cabinet Planning Secretariat in 1993 and Deputy Minister to Premiers Harcourt and Clark, he was actively involved in aboriginal issues. This background equipped him well for the intensive involvement he had with the Nisga'a file in 1998. He chaired the daily meetings of the senior management team of the larger Nisga'a Treaty Implementation Project (NTIP) team. To use a football analogy, he was clearly the veteran quarterback, the pivotal decision maker. Although interpersonal relations on the polling project were collegial or team-like, they were not egalitarian, for he clearly had the requisite power and authority to "get things done." As he noted, "I was certainly in a position where, if I felt we needed to do some polling, it would be done." Other interviewees confirmed his pre-eminent position.

John Heaney was also influential on the polling team, particularly on matters of questionnaire content. He was assistant director of NTIP and a vocal participant in the meetings of its senior management team. On the advertising campaign, his contribution was more variegated, for he was initially in charge of it, but was relegated to a lesser role when Shawn Thomas was brought on board to lead it. Heaney had prior experience on the Lubicon land claim in Alberta. He also had experience in the labour movement as Director of Research for the BC Federation of Labour, in the polling industry with the NDP's polling firm Viewpoints Research, and in a number of senior political appointee positions in government offices and central agencies, including on the Nisga'a file. He was Assistant Deputy Minister of Public Issues and Consultation, with responsibility for overseeing polling on the Nisga'a Agreement-in-Principle, which was signed on March 22, 1996. In April of 1998, when the government announced its intention to complete the Nisga'a Final Agreement within a year, he was appointed Communications Advisor to the Minister of Aboriginal Affairs and was given responsibility for the communications campaign on the Nisga'a file. Described by one interviewee (#6427) as "a totally political animal," Heaney was very much a trusted NDP insider and activist, and he and McArthur brought in other trusted NDPers, and others, to work on the Nisga'a communications initiative.

Ian Reid, Heaney's friend and one of those trusted NDP insiders, was also intimately involved. That involvement was mainly in questionnaire construction and the initial dissemination of polling results through the inner circle rather than in the advertising campaign. Reid had experience as a community organizer in Vancouver, as a ministerial assistant, and in the Policy Co-ordination Office on the management of high profile political issues. All government public opinion research was vetted through his office.

Pollster Daniel Savas, of the Angus Reid Group survey research firm, brought to the team his graduate degrees in political science and a wealth of experience in public affairs and public policy polling. Based in Vancouver, he was heavily involved in questionnaire construction and in sending results to Ian Reid. Apart from being involved in some strategizing, Savas's role was fairly circumscribed. In his words, it did not extend to "the nuts and bolts of the communications package." He did not attend NTIP senior management team meetings and travelled to Victoria only once on Nisga'a project business.

Others also were involved in the polling. However, apart from Shawn Thomas (see below), they failed to receive nomination from at least two acknowledged insiders as having been in the inner circle. For instance, the Finance Minister was consulted with regard to the appropriations for the polling and advertising, as was the Minister of Aboriginal Affairs, under whose formal mandate the polling was done. However, they were not involved in such matters as questionnaire construction and interpretation of results.

With regard to the advertising and public information campaigns, the indisputable lead player was Shawn Thomas. A political science Bachelor's graduate from Queen's University (1986) and a Master of Public Administration graduate from the University of Victoria (1991), he had worked for Glen Clark earlier. He is described further in Box 3.1

In light of how consumed provincial politics were with the Nisga'a issue during the autumn of 1998, one might expect Cabinet or a cabinet committee to have been heavily involved. However, that was not the case, for with the activity so highly centralized in the office of the Premier and his Deputy Minister, Cabinet was relatively powerless. Cabinet members reportedly were interested, but not as actively interested as they usually were when they could expect to have some influence on how an issue affected their ministry. Cabinet became more engaged when the costs of the polling and advertising campaign became a controversial public issue, but, for the most part, Cabinet was being informed, rather than consulted, on the Nisga'a campaign.

There was tension within Cabinet on the issue due to a concern there that the Premier's strategy of spending so much money on the advertising campaign was giving the issue too high a profile, polarizing it, and provoking a backlash. However, the fact that the results of the tracking surveys were generally favourable to the government's position on the Treaty militated against any cabinet interest in becoming more actively involved on the file. Said one cabinet observer,

> By and large, they felt good about what the team was doing, for sort of historic and social justice reasons, but they also felt good because they thought we were, if not winning the debate, holding our own in the debate. If your government's at 20% [support in the polls], and you get anywhere above that on an issue, you're doing well.

Twenty per cent in the polls. That very low approval rating was an important part of the political context in which the Nisga'a campaign drama unfolded. We turn to that political context in the next chapter.

The Nisga'a Treaty Implementation Project Team

The Nisga'a Treaty Implementation Project team, of which the advertising wing was just a small part, comprised some thirty-five individuals working full time on the project and another fifteen working part time (Beatty, 1998a). The team included various NDP loyalists and other non-partisan civil servants who were reputed to be outstanding at communications. One interviewee expressed his perception of the team as follows:

> [There were] a lot of very, very political people. It was a very political shop.... They weren't going to bring in just any old, like neutral civil servant. This was an intensely political initiative. And in order to be working in there, you have to be political. You had to be committed to the cause.

BOX 1.2
The "Political Administrator" and Collegial Accountability

The so-called "political administrator" is a senior public servant whose duties require trusted interaction with one or more cabinet ministers and who therefore must take political considerations fully into account in the advice that he/she proffers to the ministers.

The notion of political administrator contrasts with earlier notions of the rigid separation of politics and administration and with the doctrine of ministerial responsibility. Under those earlier notions, the minister must shield public servants from political attack and must take responsibility for the errors and scandals that occur in her department on her "watch." In return, she is entitled to the non-partisan, forthright advice of the senior public servants who report to her. Political administrators, in contrast, are likely to share the partisan leanings of their minister.

With the political administrator role come new forms of accountability. Consider, for instance, Campbell's and Szablowski's (1979) findings in their study of the "super-bureaucrats" (not all of whom were political administrators) in federal government central agencies such as the Privy Council Office, Treasury Board, and Prime Minister's Office. Campbell and Szablowski found that, among these "super-bureaucrats," norms of competitive collegial accountability prevailed over more traditional bureaucratic forms of accountability. Rooted in a desire to live up to powerful peer expectations, competitive collegiality involved

> an intense absorption in one subject or issue, continuously tested against shared mutual interests and strongly held individual opinions. It is a confident and creative approach to a particular problem originating from the desire to live up to powerful peer expectations.... Everyone, regardless of rank, is considered a peer, provided that the challenge of on-going intellectual competition is met and one "delivers the goods" when expected. In such an intense inward-oriented environment, the quality of judgments exercised by participants is always open to criticism, provided the criticism is levied according to the accepted norms of collegial professionalism. (p. 188)

Commitment to "the cause" refers to a commitment to getting the Treaty ratified. Interestingly, some who joined the Nisga'a Treaty Implementation Project team initially were not fervent supporters of the Treaty, for some were ignorant of it and some others were sceptical. Over time, though, even some of those persons reported a "conversion" experience such that they became true believers in the Treaty and were willing to endure long hours and rather poor working conditions in an old structure beside the legislature in order to get the Treaty ratified.

For those who were not NDP loyalists prior to joining the project, a definite political astuteness or sensitivity was a prerequisite for secondment to the team. Some members of the team, such as advertising "boss" Shawn Thomas, profess to this day that they strove to remain within the proper confines of the role of the non-partisan civil servant, notwithstanding how they were perceived by some others. Credence must be attached to some claims of non-partisanship, for different sources alluded to the tensions and competition within the team between "the very political NDPers" and "the non-partisan public servants," and to Doug

McArthur's task of meshing the two. Significantly, McArthur was the consummate political administrator himself.

People were seconded from a variety of locales and backgrounds in government communications, although all were trusted professionals integrated into a pre-existing network of work-based relationships. Doug McArthur was Deputy Minister to the Premier. Shawn Thomas had been at Finance, at Employment and Investment, and at BC Hydro when Clark was Minister there. (Thomas had also been a ministerial assistant during the Social Credit regime.) Thomas came to the Nisga'a team from a position as vice-president at BC Hydro and continued to work part time there while on the Nisga'a team. Don Zadravec had been at the Ministry of Employment and Investment when Shawn Thomas was there and Glen Clark was Minister. Clay Suddaby had been working as BC Ferries' spokesman, including on the controversial fast ferries portfolio. Another had been working as a communications officer to the NDP government caucus. Other interviewees who were on the team, but who do not wish to be named, were also part of Shawn Thomas's network.

Summary

The case study of the British Columbia government's selling of the Nisga'a Treaty to British Columbians, part of a larger international study of the processing of public opinion data on aboriginal issues, deals with an atypical situation wherein the focal issue is of paramount importance to the government and party in power and is given an extremely high political profile. Our understanding of the phenomenon will be enhanced by adopting and adapting the social constructionist premise that the advertising, polling, and public information campaigns are thoroughly *socio-political processes* in which meaning and significance inhere at potentially every stage. Conflict and personality clashes, far from being considered atypical or taboo, will be treated as normal social processes. Quaint notions of the separation of politics and administration will be ignored in favour of the more fruitful and true-to-life concepts of "political administrator" and "collegial accountability" (accountability to colleagues more than to bureaucratic norms). The exercise of formal and informal power will be treated as a routine fact of political life, and the political "lay of the land" will be described in detail, in terms of structure, environment, personalities, and the mystique and allure attached to polling itself.

As an analytic description or political ethnography, the book necessarily has a "split personality." In an attempt to capture the nuance, passion, and drama of history, it offers much rich description in the words of the participants themselves. However, the stories of the selling of the Nisga'a Treaty and of the polling done for Australia's Council for Aboriginal Reconciliation are not only stories of the passion, tension, and drama of men and women on a mission. Good history and good analysis necessarily also encompass the mundane, so the colourful will co-exist in these pages with more prosaic analytic exposition and historical documentation. Woven together, these different strands advance our understanding of both the public opinion polling phenomenon and the adoption of the landmark Nisga'a Treaty.

Chapter Two: "It's One of the Things I Never Know If I Should Put On My Résumés": The Political Climate

British Columbia politics are normally very intense and often highly polarized. The Nisga'a Treaty became highly politicized and is still highly politically charged. Indeed, some of those involved, including non-partisan public servants and some who are no longer in government, believe that they paid a price for their involvement;[1] others know that they did; others fear that they will. Even six years after the events, some individuals were reluctant to be interviewed or chose to remain anonymous or declined to grant permission to use some of their remarks, due to fears of politically motivated repercussions. As one interviewee (#67212) said, "It's one of the things that I never know if I should put on my résumés." An NDP insider (#0996630) alluded to the same political atmosphere when commenting on a key player in the advertising campaign, who, as he said, "has become very adept at disavowing what he used to do."

As Herbst (1998) and Foucault (1980) emphasize, power and politics are very much about local environment and context. Notwithstanding claims to the contrary, the Nisga'a Treaty polling and advertising campaigns were very much about power and politics. Therefore, this chapter describes the political climate in which the Nisga'a Treaty was set. That description explains why the NDP government escalated the politicization of the Treaty. The fact that the NDP took that politicization to the level that it did, in turn, explains why, to this day, some of those associated with the project are wary about repercussions.

Debate on the Agreement-in-Principle

After the provincial election of May 1996, which, to the surprise of many, extended the New Democratic Party's time in government for another five years, the government directed the Standing Committee on Aboriginal Affairs to hold hearings on the Nisga'a Agreement-in-Principle (AIP) and its implications for future treaties.[2] The AIP sparked intense debate, replete with opponents' allegations that it was creating "race-based government," that it was amending the Constitution,

---

1. For instance, the director of the advertising campaign, Shawn Thomas, referred only obliquely in our interview to the price that he paid. However, others reported that he was fired from BC Hydro after the Liberals came into office.
2. British Columbia Select Standing Committee on Aboriginal Affairs. (1997). *First Report, July 1997*. Retrieved April 14, 2004, from <www.legis.gov.bc.ca/cmt/36thParl/cmt01/1997/1report/process.htm>.

and that it was undemocratic in denying a vote in Nisga'a government to non-Natives who lived on Nisga'a lands. Provincially famous persons, such as talk show host Rafe Mair, former Social Credit cabinet minister Melvin H. Smith, and Liberal opposition leader Gordon Campbell, spoke out forcefully and repeatedly against it in what seemed to be a pre-emptive attempt to seize the issue from the BC Reform Party. Later, David Black (not to be confused with former newspaper magnate Conrad Black), the owner of a newspaper chain serving primarily interior British Columbia, explicitly imposed on his papers an editorial policy of opposition to the Treaty and required that a series of eight columns on the Treaty by Mel Smith be carried (British Columbia Press Council, 1999).

Debate on the AIP and the subsequent Treaty was even more highly inflamed and polarized than is true of most issues in this deeply divided province. In the style of the western frontier depicted in Hollywood movies, "Wanted!" posters, featuring MLAs who favoured the settlement, began appearing around the province. Gordon Campbell and fellow Liberal Geoff Plant eventually launched a court challenge against the Treaty itself, but had to drop it when they became Premier and Attorney General, respectively.[3]

Political Turmoil

Of particular—some would say paramount—importance was the fact that the NDP government was reeling politically at the time the Treaty was at centre stage in BC politics. Indeed, in significant part, that is why the Treaty was at centre stage at that time. The government was beset with scandal and problems and, as we shall see, the polling and advertising about the Treaty were the centrepiece of a political strategy to help the government recover. Some of the main developments contributing to the political atmosphere of the time are identified below.

Rutherdale (2002) describes the March to July 1995 legislative session in BC as one in which the NDP "lurched from one accusation or scandal to another." In March of 1995, Premier Harcourt expelled from Cabinet the Minister of Government Services, Robin Blencoe, who had been accused of sexual harassment. The following month Blencoe was expelled from caucus. A month later, Environment Minister Moe Sihota resigned after being found guilty of professional misconduct by the Law Society of BC. Although Sihota was back in Cabinet by August 1995, by December of 1996 he was forced to resign a second time amid conflict of interest allegations. In late October 1995, Harcourt fired Housing Minister Joan Smallwood, after the release of the BC Auditor General's report on the so-called "Bingogate" (Nanaimo Commonwealth Holding Society) affair confirmed that bingo proceeds had been diverted from charities to local NDP political coffers. Bingogate later claimed the political life of Premier Harcourt, who, despite not

---

3. Later, the depth of ideological opposition to the AIP and to the Treaty based on it was shown when the Reform Party of Canada sought to prevent the passage of Nisga'a Treaty enabling legislation through Parliament in April 2000 by introducing 441 amendments to it.

being personally implicated in the scandal, announced his resignation on November 15, 1995.

After the May 1996 election that returned the NDP to power, the so-called "Fudge-it Budget" scandal broke. In July, the government admitted that the $87 million budget surplus forecasted during the election campaign would actually be a deficit of as much as $235 million. In October 1996, the Auditor General announced that he would investigate the government's budget forecasting after leaked documents showed that the Ministry of Finance had forewarned the government about the problems with the provincial budget that it took into the 1996 election. A citizens' group sued the government for fraud and, in a February 1997 BC Supreme Court decision, was allowed to proceed with the case, which the group eventually lost.

Throughout the last half of the 1990s, and particularly during 1998 and 1999, the fast ferries issue was another political "hot button." In June 1994, Premier Harcourt and Employment and Investment Minister Glen Clark announced the building of three high-speed, catamaran-style ferries for the Nanaimo to Horseshoe Bay run. They were to cost $70 million each, and the first was to be "in the water" by early 1996. The ferries were completed years behind schedule, at a price more than double that first stipulated. They had to travel at less than their intended speed due to the unforeseen problem of creating a wake that was so large as to damage the shoreline when the ferries passed by. Eventually (March 2000), the NDP government admitted that the ferries were "a failed experiment" and apologized to British Columbians. The three "white elephants" were sold at a huge loss to foreign buyers for use abroad. However, during the autumn of 1998 and early part of 1999, the debacle was prominent on the Opposition's radar screen. As cost estimates escalated, calls for the Auditor General to audit the project mounted, the first ferry encountered operational problems in its October sea trials, and the newly installed president of British Columbia Ferry Services Inc. ("BC Ferries") was forced to resign in early February after only eighteen days on the job.

During the NDP's second term in office, difficult economic problems also presented themselves. For instance, 1996 has been described as the year of the collapse of the salmon fishery, hard times in forestry due to the softwood lumber dispute with the Americans, weak mining activity, and trade deficit (Hill, 2002). This was also the era of conflict with the Americans over Alaskan fishers' over-harvesting of Chinook salmon, a practice that Premier Clark condemned as costing Canadians jobs and the federal Fisheries minister condemned as damaging stocks originating in Canada.

After the Nisga'a Treaty enabling legislation was introduced in the BC legislature in autumn 1998, the political plight of the NDP took another serious turn for the worse when, on March 2, 1999, the Royal Canadian Mounted Police raided Premier Clark's home. The impending raid had been leaked to the press in advance, such that television cameras caught the highly embarrassing situation for the nightly newscasts. Criminal charges eventually were laid against him in conjunction with work done on his cottage by a contractor friend involved in seeking an application for a casino licence from the province. Although Clark was later exonerated in court, the controversy raged during part of the period in which the Treaty was being debated in the legislature. From inside the party and outside, Clark faced demands for his resignation. Four months after the April 22 ratification of the Treaty by the BC legislature, he succumbed politically and announced his resignation as Premier.

The Nisga'a Treaty as a Wedge Issue

Not surprisingly, the political turmoil that marked the NDP's time in office resulted in abysmally low levels of popularity for the party among British Columbians, as it plunged to numbers that it had not encountered even during the bleakest days of the Harcourt regime (Culbert, 1999). Apart from a brief "honeymoon" period after the 1996 election (Hunter & Ward, 1996), the party was substantially behind the Liberals throughout Clark's term as Premier.

In the election of May 1996, the NDP received 39% of the popular vote, and the Liberals received 42%. By late August of 1998, the month the Treaty was formally signed, the NDP had plummeted to 21% of decided voters, while the Liberals had 49% support. By February of 1999, NDP support had further eroded to 16% of decided voters and recovered by only two percentage points to hold steady at 18% during the spring months. Liberal Party support went as high as 59% in April of 1999, the month the Treaty was passed by the legislature. The proportion of British Columbians who approved of the Premier's performance was generally around a quarter during this period. In March of 1999, 77% of those sampled disapproved of the Premier's performance (Culbert, 1999, citing Angus Reid data).

The NDP had lost the support not only of "swing" or "middle of the road" voters but also of many—perhaps as many as half—of its core supporters. Within the party, the definition of the situation that came to prevail, among political advisors and elected politicians alike, was that the road to recovery involved recovering the core support first, and only later capturing the swing voters. Said one interviewee (#6427), "It's in that context that I believe Glen Clark 'got religion.'"

By "religion" that person was referring to Clark's commitment to the Nisga'a Treaty, for earlier in his political career, Glen Clark was not known as a champion of aboriginal land claims. The same interviewee continued,

> Glen Clark, in the run up to the 1996 election after he became leader, appeared to have little to no interest in land claims negotiations.... I think it is fair to say that his view of land claims negotiations was that it was not something that had broad based support in the province and particularly among the people he had targeted for support—what he would see as the average working person around the province....

He was not seen as an advocate for aboriginal rights at the cabinet table in any way, shape, or form while he was senior cabinet minister under Mike Harcourt. And in fact, my understanding is that he was nervous about the Nisga'a Agreement-in-Principle ... nervous about the impact that would have in what the Liberals now call "the heartland" ... in the interior, for example, places like Kamloops.... He didn't run the 1996 campaign saying "I'm going to reinvigorate the treaty process, and I want to get the first modern treaty." There's no way he's going to do that.

As noted, the Nisga'a Treaty vaulted to the top of the government's agenda during a time of political crisis within the government. The turn around in Clark's views on the Nisga'a Treaty is related to the government's casting about for an issue that would help it to win back the NDP's core base of supporters.[4] In addition, it was probably viewed by Clark as a legacy that he could leave British Columbians. To that point in the still young Clark administration, there was almost no legacy other than scandal and controversy. The same interviewee quoted previously went on to say,

> When I say "He got religion," I don't mean that too cynically.... He became, in my view, passionately committed to this. I believe that what was going through his mind was what goes through many politicians' minds, especially if they're not sure they can win another term. And they start thinking about legacy, and this was to be his legacy.... His speeches in the legislature on this were outstanding. He was genuinely moved as we went through this.... After Clark's house was raided by the RCMP, he had to know that there was a very real possibility that this was going to be it for him.

The Nisga'a Treaty came to be seen among the NDP strategists as a "wedge" issue. That is, it was seen as an issue that would not only clearly differentiate the NDP from the Liberals, but also drive a wedge among the Liberals and cause cracks to emerge in what, to that point, had been a very solid front put forth by the Liberals. The provincial Liberals were basically a coalition of federal Liberals and federal Reform Party members. The federal Reformers would be adamantly against the Treaty, and the minority of federal Liberals would be in favour of it, as was the federal Liberal government itself. Furthermore, the issue was designed to push Campbell and the Liberals farther to the right—a position that they were believed to embrace naturally. Said an interviewee who was an NDP partisan,

---

4. Not part of the present research was any consideration of the presumably substantial role played by Nisga'a leaders in educating Clark on the issue and helping to bring about the change in his orientation toward the Nisga'a Treaty in particular, and treaty settlements in general.

We had a handful of members who had been there since 1986; so, they had spent five years in opposition to the Bill Vander Zalm Socreds. And this ... cabinet minister said that the Campbell Liberals, in his view, were far more extreme in their position and views on aboriginal rights than the Bill Vander Zalm Socreds ever were.... Politically, that was part of [our] motivation—force them over to the right, make them take a position to support their right wing base that would open up space in the middle for more moderate people to see how extreme they were on aboriginal rights and perhaps think about coming back to us.... But it's my view that Clark saw this initiative as largely useless unless we got something out of it. And the only way we're going to get something out of it, like, i.e., winning people back, like increasing our support base again, would be by effectively communicating what we are doing.... If we made the Treaty popular through a massive communications effort, it would pull our numbers up even higher than just our traditional base of support.

The Nisga'a Treaty issue also served well the Premier's purposes within his caucus, his cabinet, and his party. Some members of caucus, such as the environmentalists, were unhappy with him on policy and/or stylistic grounds. For instance, some saw him as arrogant and as the "brownest" (least supportive of environmental protection) Premier in some time. However, the Nisga'a Treaty, said one observer, "was the type of issue where they would jump right on board" because it was seen as an affirmation or reaffirmation of the government's commitment to basic social democratic values. It would, in all likelihood, shore up the Premier's support among NDPers.

Another form that wedge driving can take is to encourage an elected member of a political party to defect to another party. A final indicator of the highly politically charged nature of decision making around the Nisga'a issue is to be found in Glen Clark's recruitment of Gordon Wilson, the lone Progressive Democratic Alliance member on the opposition side of the legislature, to the government side in late January 1999. Significantly, Wilson was given the Aboriginal Affairs portfolio, with responsibility for defending in the legislature both the Treaty and the government's handling of it.[5]

The Counter-Campaign

Another important element of the political environment was the opposing campaign being waged by the provincial Liberals and their allies. Their tactics included a call for a province-wide referendum on the Treaty; a barrage of letters, press

---

5. Wilson was also given responsibility for the fast ferries—an issue on which he had developed some expertise while in the Opposition.

releases, and speeches; and two high profile law suits (Palmer, 1998a)—one filed October 16, 1998 by the Fisheries Survival Coalition, federal Reform Party MP John Cummins, and others (Hall, 1998), and one filed three days later by Gordon Campbell and Geoff Plant on behalf of the Liberal Party of BC. The opponents of the Treaty also used some limited newspaper advertisements, including one that showed a government ad and attacked it, point by point. Furthermore, the Treaty's opponents had some valuable allies in the mass media, namely, popular talk show host Rafe Mair and News Group newspaper publisher David Black. As noted earlier, Black not only prohibited the papers in his chain from adopting a pro-Treaty editorial stance, but also required them to publish an eight-part series of essays written by Mel Smith in opposition to the Treaty.[6]

Not even in the same "league" as the government in terms of resources, the architects of the anti-Nisga'a Treaty campaign waged a briefer and much more circumscribed campaign than the government. Like the government's campaign, the campaign against the Treaty appealed to the value that British Columbians place upon equality and non-discrimination. Like the government's campaign, the opponents' campaign played on emotions, but, in the opponents' case, the appeal was to fear.

The opponents' advertising message was riddled with inaccuracies and distortions, which led Chief Treaty Negotiator Jack Ebbels to say, "Some of it made my blood boil!" Ebbels went on to describe the opponents' campaign as "desperate." Government officials considered it fairly easy to counter, and several of their ad messages did precisely that. The anti-Treaty campaign also was strategically flawed in another sense, which is to say that David Black's actions were turned against him by the government strategists.

Political rhetoric in public speeches was at a fever pitch. For instance, before even seeing the government's curriculum materials for elementary and high schools, Liberal leader Campbell referred to them as a government attempt to "bend young minds with their lopsided dogma about the proposed treaty" (Staffenhagen, 1998). Even pollster Angus Reid himself waded into the debate on the other side. In a speech to a federal Liberal party convention, he referred to opponents of the Treaty as the "forces of political darkness" (Rinehart, 1998a) and suggested that Campbell's demand for a referendum was the greatest act of "political stupidity" he had seen in his entire career as a pollster (Rinehart, 1998b).

In autumn 1998 and, to a lesser extent, in early 1999, politics in British Columbia were preoccupied with the Nisga'a issue. On November 30, the government took the highly unusual step of recalling the legislature for a sitting to deal exclusively with one issue—the Nisga'a Treaty.[7] However, the government's multi-million dollar campaign to sell the Treaty had already largely run its course, including intensive public opinion polling to support it. It is that polling, especially during

---

6. See Chapter Four for the details of Black's directives to his papers.

7. Debate in the legislature would be protracted, and the government finally invoked closure to bring it to an end in April 1999.

the period from mid-August 1998 to mid-November 1998, that is a prime focus of much of the remainder of this monograph. First, though, a description of the public information and advertising campaigns it fed is presented in the next two chapters. Those campaigns are somewhat of a drama themselves and shed light on how decision makers used the polling results.

Chapter Three: "Like Shovelling Money off the Back of a Truck"

It was generally seen that it wouldn't be a Chevy campaign... It was more of a Cadillac campaign.... You're pushing the high end product with the requisite resources. You weren't nickel and diming this stuff. (Interviewee #66291)

When Glen Clark was determined that something was going to happen, it happened, within government. (Interviewee #6427)

Introduction

Dick Morris is the polling advisor credited with salvaging a second term in office for Bill Clinton as President of the United States. His book, *Behind the Oval Office: Getting Re-elected Against All Odds*, which Premier Glen Clark had read, focuses in depth on polling, wedge issues, "spin," and strategy for winning back lost political support.[1] The similarities between Morris's approach and that adopted by the Clark government are striking. Although people among the "inner circle" and "key associates" said that Morris's book was by no means the "Bible" of the Nisga'a campaign, several of them had read parts of it or were otherwise familiar with it.

One of Morris's clear messages is that recovery from a serious slump in popularity requires a very effective job of communicating, which, in turn, requires massive, unprecedented amounts of advertising. Just as Morris and Clinton set out to recapture lost Democratic Party supporters, Clark became absolutely determined that the Nisga'a Treaty was to be a vehicle for recapturing the NDP's core supporters, and, as interviewee #6427 said,

> When Glen Clark was determined that something was going to happen, it happened, within government. Like I said, it was a very, very centralized structure. If the Premier wanted it, the Premier got it. And so, suddenly, it seemed like out of the blue, the major focus of government was concluding the Treaty.

Clark's political objectives were complemented by the serious anxieties of his Deputy Minister, Doug McArthur, concerning British Columbians' acceptance of

---

1. Given the 1999 publication date of the second edition, Clark probably had access only to the first (1997) edition. However, because publishers sometimes show a book's copyright date as being after its actual date of publication, it is possible that the second edition was available in the autumn of 1998.

the Treaty. McArthur had seen initial support for treaties erode over time in Yukon and Saskatchewan. Unlike BC's chief negotiator on the Treaty, Jack Ebbels, who believed that the Treaty would sell itself, McArthur was convinced that support for the Nisga'a Treaty had to be buttressed. Furthermore, as media relations specialist Don Zadravec noted, there was a belief on the implementation team that if the government did not define what Nisga'a and treaty making were all about, others would do so in their terms and to their advantage. Instead, the government would try (with mixed success, as it turned out) to set the terms of the debate, and massive advertising would be the key. The view in the inner circle, which was also conveyed to caucus, was that there is a reason that McDonalds sells so many hamburgers, and that reason is marketing. This thinking clearly held sway with the Premier, too.

Money was no object for this, the government's top priority, and approximately $7.6 million was eventually spent on the combined implementation effort, including polling, advertising, a public information campaign, and more (Canadian Press, 1998; Lavoie, 1998). The Premier felt fully justified; he was "doing the right thing" for the province. In the Nisga'a Treaty case, though, "doing the right thing" would require getting the public on side. Morris's book and others argued that one must not get too far out in front of public opinion; public opinion must be brought along. How was that to be accomplished? Said interviewee #6427,

> Not through earned media, not by hoping *The Vancouver Sun* writes nice editorials, but by running a massive advertising campaign. And so, the communications shop set up under [John Heaney] was charged with this communications task. They were given a *huge* budget.... And so, we, like, ran a ton of advertising on TV, in print, radio. It was unprecedented.

The Premier was not bashful about how much would be spent selling the Treaty to British Columbians. One interviewee suggested that a remark from earlier in Clark's career was an apt description of the mindset that guided the Nisga'a advertising campaign. When he was still Premier Harcourt's Minister of Employment and Investment, a portfolio in which he announced many government grants, Glen Clark once uttered a remark that he did not realize would be overheard by anyone in the media. It was "It's like shovelling money off the back of a truck." Said interviewee #6427,

> The reason I tell you about that is because he was very much that way about the advertising around the Nisga'a Treaty. I remember very clearly: he was boastful; he was proud; it was like shovelling money off the back of the truck, except this time we were shovelling it into Nisga'a advertising. He was conscious of the fact that ... it was the biggest advertising blitz by a BC government in the history of this province, and he thought that this was cool. It's just like when

politicians like to say "Well, this is the biggest whatever.... " Lots of politicians like, they like big.... It was like we were bringing out these big guns.

An important question can be raised at this point. Given that the government steadfastly refused to submit the Treaty to a province-wide referendum, why was a massive advertising campaign deemed necessary? The answer is that the advertising campaign was not about winning people's votes for the Treaty. In part, it was about shoring up their support for the Treaty in anticipation of the free vote in the legislature.[2] In addition, though, in significant part the campaign was about winning people back to the NDP, as noted in the earlier discussion of the Treaty as a wedge issue.

Before turning our attention to the advertising campaign, it is useful to place that advertising in context by briefly discussing the broader public information campaign waged by the Government of British Columbia.

"Leave No Shot Unanswered": The Public Information Campaign

Doug's instruction to me was to leave no shot unanswered. (Lead writer)

The resources were there; it was almost like a communicator's paradise. It was a really exciting environment for a communicator to be in. (Interviewee #66292)

Complementing the advertising campaign was a separate public information campaign. In the implementation team, it was organized under leaders responsible for media monitoring and media relations, writing, and liaising with NDP caucus members.[3] Other important components were the Premier's speeches in the legislature and his numerous speeches outside the legislature; a televised debate between the political party leaders;[4] a town-hall style discussion that featured the negotiators from the respective sides and was televised on The Knowledge Network;[5] the web site; the toll-free telephone number; approximately four hundred

2. In that respect, it is significant that the only Treaty-related polling result that the government released publicly was one showing majority support for the Treaty. It was released on the day the Treaty implementation legislation was introduced in the legislature. See Palmer (1998b).

3. The work of the MLAs was, undoubtedly, important to the government's political communication effort. However, for reasons of time and manageablility, and because the MLA liaison activities did not figure prominently in other interviewees' accounts, they were not examined in the present research.

4. See McInnes and Beatty (1998). Green Party leader Stuart Parker was excluded from the debate at NDP insistence and was forcibly removed by CBC staff when he tried to "crash" the debate.

5. Journalist Jim Beatty (1998b) reports that The Knowledge Network's parent organization, Open Learning Agency, receives $20 million annually from the BC government, including $5 million for The Knowledge Network.

public meetings; a mailing to every household in the province; brochures; displays; and two videos, one of which was intended for use in the schools.

Public demand for information on the Treaty was substantial. More than 40,000 mail outs were done, above and beyond the mail drop to each household in the province, and the toll-free information line staffed by persons from the Ministry of Aboriginal Affairs had received 18,000 calls, while the web site received 166,000 "hits," all by late January 1999.[6]

Media monitoring was not left to chance. In fact, team members were told that there was no more comprehensive media monitoring anywhere, outside of the White House. Indeed, there was nothing haphazard about any aspect of the polling, advertising, or public information campaign. Everything was carefully planned, executed, and integrated with the other elements of the strategy.

From NDP MLAs' offices, the media monitoring team would receive daily faxes of media stories, letters to the editor, interviews, commentaries, etc. In the central "war room" in Victoria, a very comprehensive daily media synopsis was prepared by Don Zadravec[7] and his three-person team and then distributed to the larger team. These summaries, approximately two and a half pages in length during mid-September, also gave a daily tally of calls to the toll-free telephone line and of visits to the web site.[8]

Operating under the maxim that no criticism of the Treaty or the government's processing of it should go unanswered, in the early days of the campaign the senior management team and lead writer would meet every weekday morning to discuss how they would respond to criticisms that surfaced in the media summaries. The meetings were chaired by Doug McArthur or, in his absence, by John Heaney. (After McArthur's departure near the end of the team's existence, his successor, Tony Penikett, former Premier of Yukon, chaired the meetings.) McArthur made the ultimate decisions on how to respond to the media coverage. Even letters to the editor had to receive his approval before going out. Later, though, as criticisms fell into a pattern and responses became more standardized, such close vetting was not undertaken. In the late stages, meetings became less frequent and focused more on larger issues, such as how to manage the problem of a particular local council that was going to pass a resolution on the Treaty.

---

6. The figures in this paragraph are taken from a contract document dated January 27,1999, but the contract does not stipulate the period covered in its tally of calls and "hits." This document was an amendment to Copeland Communications' contract with the government for the initial project (Freedom of Information Request File #292-30/AGT-2004-00143).

7. Holder of a BA and an MA in political science, Don Zadravec had held senior communications positions in a number of different government offices. Despite having worked with the Socreds early in his career, he later worked in the Premier's Office under NDP Premiers Miller and Dosanjh.

8. Specimen copies of these synopses were provided for six days in mid-September 1998, under Access to Information File #292-30/OOP-04103. The headings used in the synopses were: Dailies, Commentary, National and International Print, Regional Print, Province-wide TV, Regional TV, Province-wide Radio, Regional Radio, Ethnic Media, and Related Items (e.g., news releases from the Opposition).

The atmosphere on the team was described by some as campaign-like—very hectic and high pressure. For instance, the writing team sought to have replies sent out within twenty-four hours of the criticism's appearance, and the media relations staff was instructed to reply expeditiously to media calls. Said one of the lead members of the writing team, "It was important to be agile and ready to respond. The cycles are very quick. You either respond quickly or lose the opportunity." The media relations team leader, Don Zadravec, described the pressure another way: "Knowing that it's a priority of the government, there was a daily self-imposed pressure to not screw up.... You made a point of staying inside your message box and didn't wander far beyond it."

Despite tensions in the senior management group and their occasional flare-up into open hostility, the atmosphere was generally team-like with a definite esprit de corps—"in some ways, a bit of a SWAT team," said one interviewee (#66291). The atmosphere within the group was a complex blend of egotism, a determined and self-righteous sense of mission (a near religious zeal over doing "the right thing"), professionalism and mutual respect, profound commitment, and a sense of participating in an historic moment in the province's history. One interviewee (#67212) went so far as to compare the team to a family[9] and described an egalitarian management style: "you could have walked into that office and not known who was [boss] and who was support staff. There was no rigid pecking order." Some others did not see it that way at all and pointed to an undercurrent of tension between Heaney and Thomas or between Heaney and McArthur. For instance, one interviewee (#66292) commented, "Doug had a reputation that you had to be careful in the way you disagreed with him. You certainly couldn't challenge him." (The interviewee then went on to describe precisely such challenges.)

Egotism was an understandable human reaction to being recruited to the media relations team or the larger implementation team. Team members were assembled to work on the highest priority of the government of the day. They were recruited because they had the confidence of the Premier or of a senior person (McArthur or Thomas) who himself had the confidence of the Premier. Most had worked for the Premier in one of his earlier Cabinet postings. These individuals were considered by some to be "the best and brightest" at their line of work, and some reported that it was an "ego boost" to have been selected. However, their work generated some resentment in the Ministry of Aboriginal Affairs (e.g., the Treaty Negotiations Office) with whom both the media relations team and the senior managers had to work. Said one observer (#66292),

> The Ministry had done the heavy lifting to make the Treaty a reality. And then these perceived "Johnny-Come-Lately" political hacks came in and did the glamour work and hijacked the Treaty for political reasons and did some things in the campaign that were

---

9. Indeed, at least one family did form out of the project, as two team members who met on the team subsequently married.

counter-productive. There was some resentment there toward the implementation team.

Said another (#6630),

> When I came in there were ruffled feathers in the communications staff at the Ministry.... The perception[10] was that the Premier believed that a shoddy job had been done to date.... The mid-level and even the senior people in communications at the Ministry of Aboriginal Affairs were perceived within the communications community in government as having been pushed aside in a not very diplomatic way. My experience working with those people was that initially it was very difficult to work with them because their egos were bruised. At the time, I found it extremely frustrating because I just wanted to do the job I'd been assigned to do, and I found it difficult to get the information I needed from the place I needed to get it from—in fact, really the only source of the information.... But that was something I was able to overcome over a period of weeks or at most two months. They eventually realized I was not the person who made the decision.

John Heaney, who had major liaison responsibilities with the Ministry of Aboriginal Affairs (MAA), experienced that tension in the early days of the project, but also reported "we overcame it."

Several interviewees alluded to the sense of near-religious zeal or calling—as non-partisan Mike Krafczyk referred to it, the "higher calling"[11]—that characterized the work of many of the NDP partisans on the larger implementation team. Such zeal affected recruitment, performance, and working atmosphere. Said one person (#66292) who attended the inner circle meetings,

> Doug did want a team of "go-getters" and people with strong opinions.... There was quite a macho culture in that group and a sense of that around Clark [in terms of] looking at the world as a fight, going for the jugular, very willing to engage. He once told me that one of his favourite things was going into a really hostile scrum. This [macho orientation] was also true of some other personalities on the project.... like Heaney and McArthur.

The proactive determination accompanying that zeal and macho culture was captured in the words of the media relations team leader, Don Zadravec. Said he,

---

10. Both Heaney and McArthur disputed the accuracy of this perception.

11. Said Krafczyk, "I became quite convinced of the higher calling as I got more and more immersed in it. I became quite moved by it."

"Government was driving the bus. The bus left the station with the government firmly in charge. Those who were opposed to it were left running after the bus."

The government might have been driving the bus, but not everyone in the cavalcade always followed the same route. NDP Members of the Legislative Assembly sometimes were a source of frustration to the team in that they would stray from the aforementioned narrow message box. They frequently saw their riding as exceptional in some manner, and therefore as warranting a departure from the government's message. Writers on the implementation team would draft a letter to go out over an MLA's signature and then sometimes have to negotiate its revision with the MLA.

A more substantial, much more public, and more serious conflict emerged with the Ministry of Education in October 1998. It revolved around the issue of the placement of *optional* curriculum materials in the schools. In particular, a video was produced, and 1,700 copies had been ordered for grades four, ten, and eleven when Education officials raised strong objections. Buttressed by the Opposition, media columns, school board resistance,[12] and a wary public opinion,[13] the Ministry objected on the grounds that the curriculum was being politicized. Although the controversial video apparently was replaced with other material on the Treaty, it is significant that the Deputy Minister of Education, Don Avison, who opposed the original video, was demoted to a more junior portfolio shortly thereafter (Palmer, 1998c).

Hundreds of "town hall" meetings were held.[14] Numerous consultation meetings also were held with interest groups representing the forest industry, sport fishers, truckers, the mining association, the real estate industry, and various others. In addition, a Treaty Negotiations Advisory Committee, comprising representatives of such interest groups, was formed. It was common for the Nisga'a, the provincial government, and the federal government all to be represented at these meetings.

---

12. Sinoski (1998) reports that four of the seven members of the Surrey-White Rock school district board of trustees opposed use of the government-provided curriculum material. Surrey-White Rock is the province's second largest school district. It had an NDP-aligned faction (the Surrey Civic Electors slate), a second faction (the Surrey Electors' Team slate), and an independent trustee.

13. Reporting on a MarkTrend Research poll conducted during the period October 27 to November 2, 1998, McInnis (1998) noted that 49% of British Columbians were of the opinion that it would not be appropriate to use the video and instructional material in schools, whereas 39% felt it would be appropriate.

14. Reports of the number vary from a low of 200 in the federal government's chronology posted on the internet to "over 400" from the chief provincial negotiator to "over 500" from the federal government's Director of Public Information and Consultation.

BOX 3.1
Shawn Thomas as Seen by His Colleagues

Shawn Thomas was a pivotal person in the advertising campaign. The following are observations of him from various colleagues:

I'd never call Shawn detached. He's a very passionate individual, a real driver, someone who makes things happen. He's not a detached, neutral person.... Glen Clark pulled him in. (Peter Lanyon)

Shawn Thomas is another "alpha-dog" personality.... (#66292)

Shawn Thomas is absolutely not a New Democratic partisan. (Clay Suddaby)

The Premier totally trusted Shawn, totally.... Shawn *was* the guy—tremendous power and tremendous influence. He was basically ordained by Clark.... And Shawn's a smart guy. Shawn ran it. Shawn made every call—us coming in; how we came in; the tone, strategy, and content of ads were all dictated by Shawn.... Shawn was looking at polls every day.... If Shawn gets behind something and wants to do it, you do it.... It's not easy to stand up to Shawn Thomas; he's a very tough guy.... Shawn is like Robert Kennedy. Both were powerful, amazingly bright, outspoken (not afraid of offending anyone), front-line advisors in high-octane crises situations (e.g., Cuban missile crisis, Bay of Pigs, Nisga'a) ... Shawn is the smartest political strategist I ever met.... I think Robert Kennedy may have been recreated in Shawn Thomas. (Chuck Phillips)

Shawn had no velvet glove. (John Heaney)

If anything, the ads show Shawn Thomas's imprint—tugging at the heartstrings in ways that pass along a lesson. He makes you think.... They were five, six, seven very powerful, very bright men.... So there was some head-butting, but it was all pretty healthy. (#67212)

Assembling the Advertising Team

> This was going to be one of the biggest things that happened while Glen Clark was Premier. There was just no way that you were going to give this thing the kind of momentum it needed if you said "This little shop over here [MAA] will do it." (John Heaney)

Doug McArthur was in the "driver's seat" for the polling and the overall implementation initiative (including advertising), but, in early July 1998, Shawn Thomas was brought in to spearhead the advertising campaign.

Thomas and Peter Lanyon of the Lanyon-Phillips advertising agency had worked together on a BC Hydro campaign and were both known for producing ads that appealed to emotions. On the Nisga'a campaign, they were to work closely again, and in a similar vein.

The Ministry of Aboriginal Affairs (MAA) staff had no experience with as large a campaign as the Premier envisaged. It was a small ministry with a very small communications unit and a small budget. As John Heaney noted in the quotation at the beginning of this section, because of its small size, it was not seen as appropriate for the job.

John Heaney was initially brought in during April 1998 by the Premier's Office on contract to the Ministry of Aboriginal Affairs and given the task of overseeing the advertising, polling, and public information campaign. The only staff member on the team at first, he prepared budget submissions to Cabinet and oversaw the public tendering of the initial creative work for the advertising campaign. Copeland Communications won the competitive bidding for the advertising contract over two other firms. However, in August 1998, the Premier telephoned Heaney to tell him that he had asked Doug McArthur to take over the project. In Heaney's words, "I was in; I was out; [later] I was in again."

Why was John Heaney replaced? First, McArthur and Clark had discussed McArthur's "tremendous anxiety" (his words) about British Columbians' own anxiety over the Treaty, about the opposition campaign it would face, and about the concern that "we had all been a bit slow in getting off the mark on this." They decided that McArthur would make the Treaty his highest priority for the autumn. Secondly, unlike Heaney, who was on contract, Doug McArthur, as Deputy Minister to the Premier, carried the formal authority to tell other deputy ministers or executives of crown corporations "You *are* going to seconde these people to us" or "We *are* going to make a call upon these resources." Thirdly, the Premier had decided that he wanted a major campaign, and Heaney evidently had too modest an approach ($1.4 million) to the task, for with McArthur's appointment, the budget submissions and size of the team quickly mushroomed.[15]

The displacement of the MAA public relations staff and the displacement of John Heaney were not the only bold personnel moves made in the early days of the project. One of Shawn Thomas's early moves on the team was to remove responsibility for most of the creative communications work from Copeland Communications and bestow the lucrative job upon the Lanyon-Phillips agency. Although the matter was handled tactfully, Copeland was essentially told that its role would be confined primarily to producing print material and, in effect, serving as a conduit of funds to Lanyon-Phillips for the television ads (the so-called "glamour" work). In other words, to circumvent public tendering or other bidding requirements, Copeland was told to subcontract the television work to Lanyon-Phillips.

---

15. Heaney's own recollection was that his initial budget submission was for $1.7 million, but a planning document, dated May 1, 1998 and prepared by Copeland Communications under the title "Ministry of Aboriginal Affairs Nisga'a Treaty Campaign Cost and Timing Issues," outlines a radio, television, and mail drop communications campaign in the amount of $1,417,962 (Freedom of Information Request File #292-30/OOP-04085).

Copeland had a forceful defender in the inner circle. John Heaney, in particular, thought that Copeland had done, in his words to me, "stupendous" creative work on the pamphlet that was to go to all households in British Columbia. Nevertheless, Shawn Thomas prevailed. To smooth the potentially very troubled waters, the President of Lanyon-Phillips went to Victoria and met informally with Mike Krafczyk, Copeland's Director of Client Services on the project. In addition, Thomas and Krafczyk had a candid discussion about the importance of the work and about the fact that Lanyon-Phillips was being brought in "for the good of the project."

Copeland personnel recognized their firm's limitations. In particular, Copeland was a Victoria firm, and Victoria is not a market in which advertising firms have much opportunity to do broadcast ads. Indeed, at the time, there was only one TV station, and some of Copeland's clients had a market only on Vancouver Island. So, Copeland personnel accepted the decision graciously and continued with the responsibility for most of the print ads. They tried to be philosophical about the fact that, with the project expanding, there would be more revenue for Copeland even though Copeland would not be responsible for the television ads. Copeland did not, in any significant way, mobilize around Heaney or anyone else to resist the decision to bring in Lanyon-Phillips.

Copeland's working relations with others on the project did not become embittered or competitive; these relations merely moved into a new accommodation, and, with Thomas, they remained quite positive. Although there was little need for Copeland to work with Lanyon-Phillips, Krafczyk did try to keep Lanyon-Phillips apprised of Copeland's work. Whether due to condescension, the Vancouver-Victoria rivalry, sheer busyness, or an assumption that Thomas would be providing necessary information to Copeland, the courtesy was not reciprocated by Lanyon-Phillips. However, all indications from the interviews are that the bold move to bring Lanyon-Phillips onto the project was not accompanied by any noteworthy dysfunctionality in interpersonal relations to the point of undermining the campaign.

Shepansky Media, of Vancouver, was the advertising agency-of-record for the government and retained responsibility for placing the ads that Copeland and Lanyon-Phillips created.

Pivotal in the creative work of the campaign was Peter Lanyon. In one sense, his very conservative views (e.g., federal Conservative Party proclivities and work with the highly conservative "think tank" The Fraser Institute) and his strong initial scepticism about the Nisga'a Treaty made him a curious choice for such a key role. However, his firm, Lanyon-Phillips, had won various tenders over the years with the Clark government, and Lanyon's very conservative politics offered some protection (short lived, as it turned out) against allegations that the campaign was just NDP politicking. Probably more important, though, was the fact that, as Lanyon said, "The kind of advertising I've created has always been emotion-based, to create empathy ... and bring the people to life."

That was precisely the approach that fit with what Shawn Thomas wanted. Early on, Lanyon and Thomas met briefly with Glen Clark to share with him their creative ideas. Lanyon recalled the meeting:

> I had come with an outline of how I saw the advertising challenge and how to tackle it, but we didn't go through this and instead just had an informal conversation. My impressions of Clark were that he had considerable personable charm, affability, and warmth. His style was markedly informal and personal, and you went away liking him. He was stumping for the Treaty at the time, and I think the passage of the legislation was a real "heart and soul" matter for Glen.... I do remember his intense interest in, and enthusiasm for, what we were doing to help raise awareness of the issue and promote the Treaty's passage. It was a brief meeting, and we had his blessing to proceed.

Unlike Krafczyk, who continued with most of his responsibilities at his agency while working on the Nisga'a project, Lanyon essentially was seconded to the project. He led a small team of Lanyon-Phillips staffers on the Nisga'a work.[16] Lanyon's partner, Chuck Phillips, served in a "sounding board" (consultant) role. Occasionally, he served as a "compass" to urge that Lanyon bring the campaign back on course when it seemed to be losing its strategic direction or strategic edge. For the most part, though, Phillips ran the agency while Lanyon was immersed in the Nisga'a project as its main creative force.

Conclusion

For political, moral, and economic reasons, the Nisga'a Treaty project became a very high priority for the Clark government, as we have observed in this chapter. That Clark assigned his own Deputy Minister to the project, gave it unprecedented financial resources, brought in other such senior officials as Shawn Thomas and such trusted NDP politicos as John Heaney, met almost daily with McArthur about the project, and devoted a large portion of his own time to getting the Treaty accepted by British Columbians attests to the importance of the project in the Premier's mind. The larger, multifaceted public information campaign that complemented the advertising was conducted with a zeal and an aggressive determination that also marked the advertising campaign. It is to that advertising campaign that we now turn.

---

16. The other members of the Lanyon-Phillips team were art director Tim Kelly (on one ad), producer Melanie Lamberton who orchestrated the production crew (sound, camera, and lighting), and account director Katie Bennett. Bennett had been the account director on the ads that the agency had done for Shawn Thomas at BC Hydro. On the Nisga'a project, she used that familiarity with Thomas to offer some very frank and direct challenges to him.

Chapter Four: "It's Not About Politics": The Ad Campaign up Close

The Nisga'a Treaty is not about politics. It's about people.
(title of a full-page government newspaper advertisement)

In the previous chapters, we have seen unfold a paradox wherein the Nisga'a campaign was fuelled both by desperation politics and by the fervent belief of many of the main protagonists that ratifying the Treaty was the morally and economically right thing to do. In this chapter, we examine the advertising campaign itself more closely. In so doing, we see some of the tensions inherent in that paradox come to the fore, as the paradox itself comes into bolder relief.

Captivated by the Nisga'a: Peter Lanyon's Impact

Ad man Peter Lanyon's ideas shaped the content of the television ad campaign. A deeply spiritual person and practicing Anglican, he recalled "having my own Damascus Road experience,[1] my own change of heart." He had originally viewed the Nisga'a as a special interest group cutting a deal with government, but came to be captivated by the Nisga'a people and their spirituality, including that of Nisga'a chief Hubert McMillan, a former Anglican priest. Lanyon's remarks on this are worth quoting at length, for they go a long way toward explaining the tenor of much of the television ad campaign. They are found in Box 4.1.

The metaphor of "the journey" infused the campaign, as did Lanyon's appreciation of Nisga'a spirituality and his strategy of, in his words, "humanizing the Nisga'a to create empathy." In one very real sense, Lanyon the advertising man was, in his mind, creating the Nisga'a "brand," just as an advertiser would brand a product with an image and then market that image. His business partner, Chuck Phillips, very much saw the campaign in those terms. Perhaps self-conscious about connotations of the commodification of the Nisga'a, Lanyon himself shied away from describing the strategy as one of marketing a Nisga'a "brand." However, he did make the following admission:

> I did see it as having some of those things—the Treaty had to stand for something; we had to give a face to it; we had to give a person-

---

1. The reference is to the biblical story (Acts 9:1–9) of the conversion experience of Saul on the road from Jerusalem to Damascus five years after the death of Christ. Saul had been vigorously persecuting Christians but on the road to Damascus saw a brilliant light and heard a voice saying "Saul! Saul! Why do you persecute me? ... I am Jesus, the one you are persecuting."

BOX 4.1
Peter Lanyon's Journey

I thought that if I had to go up there [to Nisga'a territory] to experience that change, then I should take British Columbians through the same kind of experience I had had. It is not enough to communicate just with the head. You must speak to the heart.... I got this quote out for you from Jean Chrétien in his book *Straight From the Heart*: "The public is moved by mood more than logic, instinct more than reason, and every politician must make use of, or guard against, that."

I am a very spiritual person. The spirituality of the Nisga'a people really connected with me. I was very, very deeply impressed by them, especially by the old chief, Hubert McMillan who spoke in the Nisga'a language. He had this tremendous spiritual authority.

The Nisga'a are like the Dalai Lama, not like militant Native groups. I was very struck by their spirituality, dignity, and sense of patience. They were never hard-hearted or blaming or pointing fingers. I wanted British Columbians to experience the same kind of personal change that I had—to see them as people, real people, not just out to get something from government.

—Peter Lanyon

---

ality to the Nisga'a people and the Treaty for people to empathize with that cause. But it certainly was not like a McDonald's campaign—not too heavy handed. It didn't look overly packaged.

While the Nisga'a people undoubtedly did not see themselves as lacking a face or personality or humanity, Lanyon's belief was that, in the minds of British Columbians, the Nisga'a did not have a face and personality that differentiated them from other Natives in BC, such as the militants and the stereotypical "skid row bums." So, within days of being hired in August 1998, Lanyon was off on the first of two visits to New Aiyansh in Nisga'a territory to begin shooting interview and other footage of the Nisga'a people in their own setting. That footage would become a large part of an eighteen-minute video called *A New Journey*, which was shown on The Knowledge Network and The History Channel. Describing that video, Lanyon recalled the tight time constraints under which he was working and how that affected the work:

There was a great deal of stuff to put together in a very short period of time without the usual pre-planning, in comparison to a few months to do a similar commercial campaign. It was like "Ready. Fire. Aim." I was growing organically what I would do [as I went along].... It was jumping in, both feet. With the commercials, though, we had more time.

Shawn Thomas also remembered very tight time constraints. Said he, "We broke so many records ... It's just astounding how fast it was done."

Objectives and Strategy of the Advertising Campaign

The political objectives of driving a wedge between the two parts of the coalition that comprise the provincial Liberal Party and recapturing lost NDP support by differentiating the NDP from the Liberals have already been discussed. They were widely acknowledged by interviewees. There were also other objectives. John Heaney described the objective of the advertising campaign as being to inform people about the Treaty and to create the political and social will to see it ratified, such that legislators could vote in favour of the Treaty with confidence that, at that point in history, they had the support of their constituents. This last objective required, in his view, a campaign that identified the Treaty's societal, economic, and individual benefits.

Despite frequently being at loggerheads with Heaney, Shawn Thomas described the objectives of the campaign in similar terms—namely, to create broad public awareness of the Treaty, to stimulate public debate, and to stimulate both acceptance of the Treaty and an awareness of the benefits of signing it and moving forward with other treaty settlements throughout the province. He also noted the longer term objectives of the campaign and alluded to the fact that they could take on distinctively political overtones:

> This wasn't just about Nisga'a; it was also about other treaties—about using the Nisga'a Treaty and the success of it to try to communicate and promote throughout the province the whole notion of treaties, in general, and getting treaties settled and the need for public consent and support, and start getting other treaties and other successes. So it really was about a platform for going forward, as much as it was about the Nisga'a Treaty itself. And some of the challenge came around how to do that because that was seen as moving into the realm of [the] political, and some of us had a concern about doing that.... When it came to issues of wedge and differentiation and politics, where it was one government or party against another, a lot of us put our hands up and said, "We'll not be a part of that. It would not be appropriate for us to be a part of that."[2]

The strategy for achieving the objectives was a matter of considerable disagreement within the team. Creative director Peter Lanyon was in favour of a highly emotional campaign that evoked empathy for the Nisga'a people, in combination with a more facts-oriented component. Copeland Communications had

---

2. Although Thomas elsewhere described himself as having become the voice of the nonpartisan public servants on the team, his statement here is ambiguous as to whether he himself was among the "some of us" who resisted the politicization of their work. Recall the comments of Clay Suddaby in Box 3.1. John Heaney, who in some respects was Thomas's foil on the campaign, when explicitly asked, was another who did not categorize Thomas among the NDP partisans.

already laid down the informational layer in the campaign—pamphlets and fact-heavy print advertising—before the Lanyon-Phillips agency was engaged. Said Lanyon,

> We were brought in to help raise the visibility of the issue on the public agenda and add an emotional layer to the communications. To me, the key was to take the Treaty beyond a piece of polemical NDP legislation, with arguments pro and con, to a more party-neutral cause, a more humanitarian cause, that could attract and motivate a cross-section of voters.
>
> I have always believed emotions are key drivers of attitudes, motivation, and choice. I thought the best route to create positive attitudes and support for the Treaty was to reach people emotionally.
>
> That in mind, there were two prongs to the creative strategy: (1) create empathy for the Nisga'a ... we had to get voters to see them as a people, rather than a faceless issue, and kindle empathy for their cause.... and (2) create a sense of wide, thoughtful support and building momentum for the Treaty. This involved filming interviews with various community and thought leaders in BC.

That two-pronged approach prevailed. As the campaign evolved, the empathy strategy was pursued through the use of what is known in the industry as "high production values." More specifically, that involved use of cameras that move, sophisticated camera angles, multiple "exotic" locations (rather than being confined to a studio), many people, and the use of music. Shawn Thomas, who regarded Lanyon-Phillips as "probably one of the most powerful creative ad agencies in Canada," backed Lanyon fully in this approach and insulated him from the debate in the inner circle by not asking him to the inner circle's meetings.

John Heaney was a forceful voice for proponents of a very different strategy. Not only had he not wanted the Copeland agency supplanted by Lanyon-Phillips, he also favoured a strategy of appealing to British Columbians' self-interest in the treaties, rather than appealing to their emotions as Lanyon-Phillips was proposing. Said Heaney,

> We wanted to make a persuasive argument that British Columbia had been a place that was disadvantaged by the failure of previous governments to resolve the aboriginal land question and that we were suffering economically, socially, spiritually, and that this represented an opportunity to reconcile some of those problems of the past, that we might never get another chance, and furthermore, that people could identify their self-interest in [this Treaty].

Heaney's preferred strategy was rooted in the conviction that the persons with whom Lanyon's "emotional" approach would resonate well were precisely the people who were already "on board." Lanyon's approach, Heaney believed, failed to move the main target audience. Heaney elaborated,

> [Chief] Joe Gosnell's a beautiful man, and he's one of my favourite British Columbians, but when Lanyon-Phillips took on this file and went up to the Nass [River valley in Nisga'a territory] and ran ads that cost a lot of money to make in 35 millimetre film with lush production values of Joe in a wooded forest, wearing his traditional regalia, and flying over the land, and all this sort of stuff, and saying "It's time"—great, it's wonderful.... That ad, it was beautiful; it was gorgeous; it made me cry. But it was ineffective because the audience that it was aimed at was already onside, and the lushness of it "dripped" money and made the people we were trying to win over in the middle on [the basis of arguments that] it's affordable, it's doable, it's good for the economy—it drove them away.

Shawn Thomas and Peter Lanyon carried out their strategy by using the print material and some radio ads to convey the facts of the situation—such as the amount of land involved and the type of powers to be held by the Nisga'a government—while television was used to raise awareness and stimulate debate by appealing to (primarily positive) emotions[3] about aboriginal issues. The view was that advertising in print media works best when used in support of electronic media and that neither works very well without the support of "earned" media—news coverage of proponents making the case for the Treaty.

"You'd Have Had To Be Living Under a Rock": Words, Images, and Weight of the Advertising Campaign

The ad campaign was far-reaching, intensive, and multifaceted . As Don Zadravec observed, "You'd have had to have been living under a rock sometimes, not to have seen a TV ad for Nisga'a." Said one of his colleagues from the writing team, "The whole ad campaign was saturation. You couldn't get away from Nisga'a." When asked whether he was ever told "Give me a Coca-Cola campaign" or "I want a McDonald's type of campaign," Shawn Thomas replied,

> Yes, I was told that they wanted such a campaign, in terms of weight [air time bought]. We wanted people to see a number of commercials a number of times. So the decision was made, if we need to create high public awareness, we need to put weight behind the television buy.... And I remember having conversations around, yeah, McDonald's.

---

3. Interestingly, the material that some found so emotionally moving and the Opposition criticized as emotionally manipulative struck this observer as relatively bland. Lanyon reported that the focus groups did not find the ads to be emotionally manipulative.

The ad campaign comprised radio and television ads, newspaper ads, pamphlets made available on the BC ferries and to BC municipalities, and a pamphlet mailed to every household in British Columbia. The eighteen-minute video entitled *A New Journey*, from which some of the TV ad material was taken, was also shown on television. While our consideration of the ads is hampered by the unavailability of some of them and by memory loss among participants, enough specimens and information on them were obtained to permit a useful description of the campaign.[4]

Television Ads

The television ads were of three main types. The first type were the aforementioned "high production value" ads that featured Nisga'a leaders and other Nisga'a individuals speaking about the situation of the Nisga'a people and/or the Treaty. Images of Nisga'a children and the stunning beauty of the Nisga'a landscape were also incorporated into this first type of ad.[5] The second type featured non-Native opinion leader "celebrities," such as environmental scientist Dr. David Suzuki, former BC Federation of Labour president and then Forest Alliance of BC chairman Jack Munro, and economist Roslyn Kunin of the Laurier Institute "think tank." (Attempts to get celebrities Sarah McLaughlin and Rick Hansen were not successful.) The third type of television ad was the so-called "rolling super" ad, which is to say white script superimposed on a black background and read by a narrator while the script scrolled ahead. There were two ads of this last type, and they were featured at the end of the television campaign. The same technique was featured in the video *A New Journey*.

The thirty- and sixty-second television ads were intended to run province-wide from August 4, the day of the formal signing ceremony in New Aiyansh. However, records indicate that start was delayed to August 10 because the creative material was not ready. Those initial ads, requisitioned by Copeland Communications, ran for two weeks.[6] The next batch of ads ran from October 5 for four weeks. Plans to run them during the middle two weeks of November were cancelled due

---

4. My efforts to procure the television ads were only partly successful, although I did view three and the entire *A New Journey* video, from which some other ads were taken.

5. For another example of First Nation people themselves incorporating landscape as a vehicle of highly politicized discourse on another aboriginal issue of national importance—the Oka dispute—see Ponting (1991).

6. Copeland went to New Aiyansh and filmed some black and white footage. My interviewees' memories were "fuzzy" on dates and details, but it appears that the first TV ads requisitioned might have been created by Copeland. John Heaney authorized the expenditure, dated July 24, 1998. This would be consistent with his recollection that it was in August that the Premier put Doug McArthur in charge of the project and with Peter Lanyon's recollection that he didn't come on the project until the end of August. Cancellation records show that an unsuccessful attempt was made on July 29 to cancel the initial two-week television buy that was to run beginning August 4. This cancellation attempt might have been due to the creative material not being ready.

to a provincial by-election. TV ads also ran only in the regions outside Victoria and the lower mainland for a week beginning November 23.

The placement of these various TV ads was exceptional, for they ran during popular shows like *South Park, Friends,* and *Hockey Night in Canada.* McArthur recalled that there was some debate about "whether we were getting the best 'bang' in our placements." He added, "I had some arguments with Shawn about placements, but in the end it was Shawn's call. I think our argument was about the time of day.... I'd have been a fool to inject myself in that kind of stuff."

Appendix 5 provides a description of a sixty-second ad, featuring David Suzuki, with which the Lanyon-Phillips agency was particularly pleased.[7] The spoken text captures the ad campaign's appeal to values of justice and patience, and also demonstrates the emphasis on the dignity of the Nisga'a people. The visual images not only captured aspects of the rich Nisga'a culture and spirituality that had so captivated Peter Lanyon but also appealed both to the value that Canadians place on children and to British Columbians' ties to the natural environment. The musical track featured Native singing and drumming. Said Chuck Phillips,

> The David Suzuki piece was probably the most powerful piece of advertising we'd ever done in twelve years. He was amazing.... We took him to Stanley Park. We put a script outline together, and he didn't need that because he was speaking from the heart. It was really an emotional issue for him, and that emotion came out.... [That ad] speaks for itself. I don't need to tell you how much power it had. I think it had a lot of influence with anybody who would have seen that.

Radio Ads

Two main types of radio ads could be identified. The first type comprised simple 30-second public information announcements that informed listeners of a public information forum that would be taking place in their community. An example was the ad for the forum with BC Aboriginal Affairs Minister Dale Lovick and federal, provincial, and Nisga'a negotiators, held September 15, 1998 at the Northwest Community College campus in Terrace and sponsored by the College and the provincial government. The second type of radio ad might be called the "Know the Facts" ads. Written by Peter Lanyon, these 30-second spots all began with the sentence "It's important that all British Columbians know the facts about the Nisga'a Treaty" and ended with "The Nisga'a Treaty. A message from the province of British Columbia. For more information, call 1-800-880-1022." Inserted between this standard opening and closing would be one of the nine "facts"

---

7. At time of writing, this ad could be viewed on Peter Lanyon's web site at <www.peterlanyon.ca>.

messages shown in Box 4.2. Background music and sound effects (e.g., chirping birds) played while the narrator read the ad.

The "Know the Facts" radio advertising campaign, which was initially billed at $629,619.98 (including air time and the Shapanski agency's fee of approximately 2.6%), was scheduled to run during the period September 14 through November 15, but was extended to the end of November at an approximate cost of an additional $195,000.[8] It ran throughout the province. The initial requisition demonstrated a clear intent to leave no corner of the province untouched by these ads, for they were placed with 59 radio stations outside Vancouver and with various Vancouver stations.[9] The saturation coverage is further demonstrated by the fact that, in most of the markets outside Vancouver, the initial requisition alone called for a buy of 315 thirty-second spots per station over the eight-week period. For instance, in the northeastern community of Chetwynd, radio station CHET-FM was to play Nisga'a ads in 40 spots in each of the two weeks beginning September 14, 1998, in 35 spots in each of the next three weeks, in 30 spots in each of the three weeks beginning October 19, and in 40 spots in the week beginning November 9, for a total of 315 spots.[10]

Print Media Ads

The print media campaign was more diverse than the radio spots. Some print ads were a simple announcement of a public information forum. Others, in the *TV Times* television program listings or as a quarter page in the main body of the newspaper, were a fairly straightforward announcement of the time and channel on which the *A New Journey* video, identified as having been produced for the Province of British Columbia, would be shown.[11] Another, which ran in mid-August 1998, highlighted a toll-free telephone number that readers were invited to phone to leave a comment, to order a copy of the Treaty, or to speak directly with a Ministry of Aboriginal Affairs staff member. Interestingly, this early ad

---

8. These figures are taken from Advertising Placement Order (APO) #08710 (September 15, 1998) and APO #09914 (December 17, 1998) obtained under Freedom of Information request, File 292-30/OOP-04085. APO #09914 suggests that the supplemental cost might have been $255,000, rather than $195,000. When cancellations occurred, the government was sometimes able to recover some of the funds committed or transfer the purchased advertising time to another ministry for its purposes. Thus, it is better to work with rounded numbers, rather than precise numbers, when tallying the cost of the Nisga'a campaign.

9. Of the initial almost $630,000 requisitioned, about $228,000 was for Vancouver stations that were unspecified in the requisition, except for the $25,525.50 for three Vancouver Chinese stations.

10. The increased frequency in November is probably indicative of an early expectation that the Treaty would face the ratification vote in the legislature around that time.

11. The government paid for the showing of *A New Journey* on The History Channel and, presumably, on The Knowledge Network. The cancellation of the November 15 showing on The History Channel saved slightly under $3,600 (less $91 because of Shepansky's fee for handling the cancellation).

BOX 4.2
"Facts" Messages in the 30-Second Radio Ads

- KMPG and Price Waterhouse, two national accounting firms, say that having no Treaty and the resulting uncertainty surrounding unresolved land claims, have already cost our province over a billion dollars in lost investment and jobs.
- Canada prides itself on protecting minority rights. Issues like the Nisga'a Treaty have traditionally been dealt with in the legislature and Parliament, by elected representatives responsible to you. Each member of the BC legislature will be free to vote their conscience and reflect on the wishes of the people they represent.
- Under the Treaty, private property owned by non-Nisga'as on Nisga'a land will be fully protected. Private land is not part of the Nisga'a Final Agreement and will not be on the table in any treaties the BC government negotiates.
- Under the Treaty, the Nisga'a will receive $312 million over 15 years to invest in education, job training and business development, and to help them become self-supporting taxpayers. Of that cost, BC will pay one fifth; Canada combined pays four fifths.
- Under the Treaty, special status for the Nisga'a people will be eliminated. Because the Nisga'a will cease to be governed by the federal Indian Act, they will now be required to pay taxes. They'll also be subject to the Canadian Constitution, the Charter of Rights and Freedoms, and federal and provincial laws, like other British Columbians.
- Talks with the Nisga'a began in the early 1900s. In recent times, three different BC governments and thousands of British Columbians have had input. There have been over 400 public meetings held and the details of the initial agreement have been widely available since 1996.
- Under the Treaty, the total land to be returned to the Nisga'a is 2,000 square kilometres, one tenth of their original land claim. And the maximum land under discussion in all First Nations treaties is only 5% of the province, an amount proportional to their population.
- When the Treaty goes to our legislators in Victoria, they'll be allowed to cast a free vote, according to their conscience and not along party lines. When they cast their vote, they'll be reflecting on your opinion. Another vote will be held in our federal parliament. And the Nisga'a will hold their own ratification vote.
- Under the Treaty, the Nisga'a people are allowed to govern themselves like a local, municipal government, in areas like traffic, zoning and police. But they are subject to the Canadian Constitution, The Charter of Rights and Freedoms, the Criminal Code, and other federal and provincial laws.

Source: Radio transcripts obtained through Freedom of Information request, File 292-30/OOP-04053.

also presaged the political tone that the campaign was to take. After identifying some of the benefits of the Treaty and declaring "It's time to resolve aboriginal land claims. It's time to agree—to a better future," the ad closed with the BC government logo above the slogan "Bringing BC Together" and the invitation to visit the web site.

Some other ads that ran in the print media ran under the title "The Nisga'a Treaty: What Does It Mean To Me?" These featured a striking aerial photo depicting a river (probably the Nass) running through a dense forest toward hills or mountains in the background. Superimposed on this scene were some brief

BOX 4.3
Content of the "It's Not About Politics" Ad

The Nisga'a Treaty
is not about politics.
It's about people.

It's about a people who lost the land of their ancestors without ever signing a treaty.

It's about a people who saw their children taken away to residential schools, their culture systematically dismantled and their families decimated by the ravages of disease, alcohol and dysfunction.

It's about a people who must live on government handouts, in third world conditions, in one of the most prosperous nations on earth.

It's about a people who do not enjoy rights other Canadians take for granted. The right to own the property their houses sit on. To make a will without the consent of bureaucrats. To control their own assets.

It's about a people who are still subject to government under an antiquated Indian Act and a reservation system that was the model for Apartheid.

It's about a people who have negotiated peacefully, patiently, and in good faith, for over 111 years, with governments of all political stripes, to bring closure to the issue of land claims. To settle things once and for all, in accordance with the decision of the Supreme Court of Canada.

And it's about a people who, in spite of everything, still desperately want to be part of this country and are prepared to surrender over ninety percent of their traditional territories and their personal tax exempt status to achieve that dream and take their place as equals in Canadian society.

The Nisga'a Treaty is not about politics.

It's about people. It's about justice. And it's about time.

[BC logo]

British Columbia
Glen Clark, Premier

questions with brief answers. For instance, one ad, which ran around September 23, contained the questions "Is private property on the table?", "Will my taxes go up to pay for this?", and "Will the Nisga'a pay taxes just like me?" Another ad of this type, which ran in mid-October, contained the questions "Does the Treaty create a separate Nisga'a nation?", "Is there a cost to delaying treaties?", and "Do I get a say in the Treaty?" The toll-free phone number and web site address were also included in these ads, along with the BC government logo.

BOX 4.4
Values to Which the Government Ads Appealed

An examination of the content of the ads reveals numerous different values with which the ads would resonate in the target audience. In many respects, the ads of the government and the opponents appealed to the same values.

Security was an important value that was tapped. The opponents of the Treaty waged a campaign based upon fear, and the government ads sought to alleviate those fears, such as the fear that private property owned by "third parties" would be lost under the Treaty. Like the opponents, the government ads appealed to the value that British Columbians attach to *equality*. In the government's case, this took the form of emphasizing ways in which the Treaty eliminated "special status" for the Nisga'a. Both sides also appealed to *democracy* as a value. Whereas the opponents approached this in terms of their demand for a referendum on the Treaty, the government replied with the offer of a free vote in the legislature. *Economic affordability and stability* were also prominent themes used by both sides. The opponents argued that BC could not afford the Treaty, while the government pointed to a consultant's report that estimated that over one billion dollars of investment in BC had already been lost because of the uncertainty surrounding unsettled land claims. Thus, *certainty* (predictability) itself was a value to which the government appealed.

Perhaps foremost in the government's campaign was the value of *fairness* or *justice*. As Box 4.3 demonstrates, the ad campaign placed great emphasis upon the notion of rectifying a longstanding injustice. *Timeliness* was another value underlying the government's campaign, as the government asserted that the talking had gone on long enough, and the time to resolve the issue was at hand.

Yet other print ads ran under the heading "The Facts About The Nisga'a Treaty." After each of seven different sub-headings, one to four brief "statements of fact" were presented. For instance, one such ad, which ran just after Labour Day, addressed tax equality, the land, the Nisga'a government, a free vote, a public process, a cost shared by all Canadians, and economic certainty. As always, the toll-free telephone number and web site address were included.

Another print ad, which ran on November 13, was entitled "The Nisga'a Treaty is Not About Politics. It's About People." It was the only print ad done by Lanyon-Phillips. Like some of the others, it was a full-page ad. It was noteworthy also for its lack of any graphics and for the fact that it was signed by the Premier. Its content is reproduced in Box 4.3 and on Lanyon's website.

The penetration of these and other ads throughout the province was phenomenal. Appendix 4 provides the schedule of government newspaper and magazine advertisements on the Treaty. Although some modifications were made to this intended schedule, it does portray well the scope of the newspaper and magazine campaign. It shows that ads were placed in 19 daily newspapers, 24 ethnic newspapers (including nine in translation involving several different languages), 7 aboriginal publications, 2 "alternate" publications like *The Georgia Straight*, 12 campus publications, 150 community newspapers (many of which were part of the chain owned by publisher David Black), and 5 business magazines.

The Video "A New Journey"

The Lanyon-Phillips full-colour video entitled *A New Journey: The Nisga'a Treaty* was a centrepiece of the advertising campaign. As noted, some footage from it, such as one of David Suzuki's five segments, was used for the television spot ads. It captured most of the values to which the campaign appealed and was a clear exemplar of the highly emotive, high production values approach that Lanyon and Thomas "sold" to Glen Clark. Using images of beautiful landscape (e.g., rivers and idyllic waters), children, on-reserve poverty, the Nisga'a as Canadians, and the vibrant traditional culture of the Nisga'a that survives in contemporary times, the video made the case that the Nisga'a had been subjected to injustice and that the time to rectify that injustice is now. It also addressed stereotypes of aboriginal people, arguments used by opponents of the Treaty, and the strong points of the proponents' arguments. It used spokespersons such as Nisga'a leaders and other Nisga'a individuals (the mid-August polling showed that these were the two types of spokespersons from whom British Columbians most wanted to hear about the Treaty) and others with high credibility, such as David Suzuki, Jack Munro, Chief Treaty Negotiator Jack Ebbels, and the Laurier Institute's Roslyn Kunin.

The David Black Controversy

Opposition to the Treaty, and to the Agreement-in-Principle before it, was described in Chapter Two as part of the account of the "counter-campaign." Here we examine briefly the controversial directive of News Group publisher David Black, in terms of its effect upon the government's campaign. Black, it should be noted, owns over fifty newspapers in BC and a few outside the province. His BC holdings comprise various suburban community papers and dozens of non-daily newspapers in the BC interior, including most of those in the province's northwest, the area most affected by the Treaty. He continued his acquisitions during the Nisga'a campaign with the September purchase of two Okanagan dailies: the *Penticton Herald* and the *Kelowna Courier*.

Black's directives to his editors, as presented in evidence to a BC Press Council hearing, were as follows: (1) The editorial position of the David Black newspapers was to oppose the proposed Nisga'a Treaty; (2) A series of eight columns on the subject by Mel Smith would be run by all David Black newspapers; (3) Existing columnists were free to disagree with the owner's position within their columns; (4) Letters to the editor and news reporting were not to be affected; (5) Editors who disagreed with the owner's policy were not obliged to write against their conscience but would be expected to run material provided to them; and (6) Editors who disagreed with the owner's policy were free to express their thoughts on the letters page (British Columbia Press Council, 1999).

That directive initially caused great alarm in the government's war room. John Heaney recalls the day,

Everyone had his knickers in a knot. —— was lighting his hair on fire, saying "This is a disaster. It's the elite coming after us. How are we going to fight back on this? They own newspapers; all we own is tax dollars to buy ads." He was perturbed, very perturbed.

Heaney did not share that sense of alarm. Instead, he regarded Black's actions as an opportunity, as actually the best thing that had happened to date in the government's campaign. He recalls arguing,

> We're finally going to get some traction and some notice, and David Black is going to be the guy who characterizes opposition to this campaign. His ideas are not in step with the middle of the audience we're targeting, and the fact that he is forcing local editors to run his editorials sullies that side of the debate. We couldn't have asked for a greater gift.

Another participant (#66292) commented in a similar vein: "Black was trying to stifle debate. This was manna from heaven for the political minds involved [on our team]."

In Heaney's words, "We took a hard run at him, and David Black hurt the 'No' side." A hard run, indeed! The Premier met with Black in Vancouver and tried unsuccessfully to change his mind. Then he debated Black on a spirited open-line radio show. Eventually, the government filed a complaint about Black's actions with the BC Press Council. Newspaper columnists, editorialists,[12] and Native leaders[13] also became involved in issuing harsh critiques of Black's actions.

The rhetoric, of course, was ratcheted up a notch, as Clark called Black's order to his editors a "naked abuse of trust," which Black holds as a publisher of a newspaper (Griffin, 1998). Clark was also reported (Griffin, 1998) as saying that Black's position shows the danger of corporate concentration of the media and that his newspapers aren't really community papers at all, but are owned by one person who feels he has the right to impose his views on the public. BC Native leader Grand Chief Ed John, speaking on behalf of the First Nations Summit, asserted that Black's "directive to dictate editorial policy and ban rebuttal articles flies in the face of one of the fundamental tenets of any democracy—free speech. It is as if we were back in the Wild West again" (Griffin, 1998).

Significantly, the government chose not to pull its ads from Black's newspapers.[14] To do so would have appeared petty and vindictive, would have reinforced the view that the Nisga'a campaign is "about politics," and would have

---

12. For examples of newspaper commentary on Black's edict, see Easingwood (1998) and Leyne (1998).

13. See Griffin (1998).

14. Nevertheless, Black reported that his stance was costing him economically as some other advertisers, fearful of aboriginal economic reprisals, were staying away from his papers. See Hogben (1998).

reduced the government's access to Black's readers. Instead, with a determination to turn Black's actions to the government's advantage, the government challenged Black directly, forcefully, and repeatedly. That challenge itself generated much "earned" media coverage. Said one NDP partisan, "We got gallons and gallons of ink spilled on this story." By the time the Press Council announced its decision on January 15, 1999, it mattered little that the government's complaint was not upheld by the Council.

Getting Back on Track

As already noted, within the inner circle there was intense disagreement over the wisdom of using the emotionally evocative, high production value ads. Those expensive ads also came under attack in the caucus, Cabinet, press, and, of course, from the Opposition. Heaney was not successful in blocking those ads or some others, for after Thomas came on the team, Heaney's role was curtailed. Heaney did vet the mock-up print ads for accuracy and checked them out with the Ministry of Aboriginal Affairs. He also reports that the senior management group saw or heard almost all broadcast ads before they went to air. However, he also noted that, at its morning meetings, the senior management group was shown some television ads only at the "eleventh hour." Commenting on the radio and television ads that came to the morning meetings, he said,

> We were able to stop some things before they went to air, [but] we were shown some things that would be on BC TV that night. We stopped a [radio] ad with a tag line "The Nisga'a Treaty. Think about it." It was up to me to "bell the cat." It [the tag line] is a disaster. It implies people haven't been thinking about it. It's confrontational.

Thus, Thomas and Lanyon had a relatively free hand on the creative side, although the Premier and his Deputy both took a very active interest in the ads. Eventually, though, the Thomas-Lanyon approach proved unsustainable in the face of the widespread criticism, disconcerting polling results,[15] and feedback from both the MLAs and the Outreach team. Lanyon's partner, Chuck Phillips, came to believe that the campaign had not only become too spiritual, too artistic, and too expensive in appearance, but also had become too defensive. He and Thomas prevailed upon Lanyon to bring the campaign "back on track." Said Phillips, "When it got too fuzzy, too soft, it was Shawn who said, 'We're stopping that direction and coming back.' And he was looking at polls every minute on this thing."

---

15. In addition to the implementation project's own polling, a published poll by MarkTrend Research suggested that part of the advertising campaign was counter-productive. For instance, 26% of the 502 British Columbians surveyed between October 27 and November 2, 1998 said that they were less likely to support the Treaty after seeing the government ads, while only 18% said they were more likely to support the Treaty, and 53% said that the ads had no effect on them. See McInnes (1998).

Getting the campaign "back on track" involved running the "rolling supers" ads on television and the newspaper ad entitled "The Nisga'a Treaty is not about politics" (see Box 4.3). Lanyon wrote the full-page ad and submitted it to Thomas, who took it to the Premier. It went to print without a change, Lanyon recalled. Reflecting on that ad six years later, he cited it as one of the two things of which he was most proud in the Nisga'a campaign. He wrote to me:

> [B]etter than anything else, it summed up the overall approach (emotional/factual) and created just the right balance between fact and emotion. Years later, I showed the ad to Roy Henry Vickers, the great BC native artist. He read it and cried. I think that piece may have touched a lot of people.

Glen Clark's Role and Who Was "Calling the Shots"?

Glen Clark was a colourful, opinionated, highly intelligent, aggressive, skilled politician. He came to hold (and act upon) strong ideas about the Nisga'a Treaty's place in the moral, political, and economic universe of British Columbia. For the Nisga'a Treaty Implementation Project he was actively involved in some key decisions of prioritization, overall strategy, and resourcing, and even in two personnel decisions.

However, contrary to what some participants believed, Glen Clark did not "hand pick" the key members of the implementation team, with the exception of Doug McArthur and Shawn Thomas. It was McArthur who selected the other key team leaders, and it was Thomas who selected the Lanyon-Phillips advertising agency. Said McArthur about that decision, "We never canvassed that at any level. It was Shawn's decision. I would have had no interest. I don't know those [advertising] guys one from another."

Premier Clark was heavily involved in the symbolic work of the ratification of the Treaty, and wanted to become even more involved. He campaigned widely and vigorously for the Treaty within the province and in Toronto and Ottawa, and was its staunch defender in the BC legislature and in a televised leaders' debate on the Treaty. As we shall see later in this book, he was intimately involved in poring through polling results. Furthermore, he became personally involved in vetting advertisements, he met on a number of occasions with Shawn Thomas, and the "It's not about politics" ad was published over his signature. He was even featured in one television advertisement that the Lanyon-Phillips agency shot in his Victoria office. However, after great debate within the inner circle, the decision was taken not to use that ad.[16]

---

16. The reasoning was that although the Premier was perhaps the Treaty's most articulate proponent, featuring him in a commercial risked identifying the Treaty with him and miring it in partisan politics.

For the most part, Glen Clark was not "calling the shots" on the Nisga'a file, for he assigned to the project experienced professionals in whom he had absolute trust and confidence. He kept closely informed, and assumed a high public profile in the selling of the Treaty, but he left the day-to-day management of the portfolio to McArthur. As McArthur said, "I made the decisions, with Shawn, on all the ads, in terms of content, timing, etc."

Assessment of the Advertising Campaign

Despite the availability of polling data, the advertising campaign is difficult to assess. Indeed, different participants view it differently. John Heaney, for instance, saw the emotion-oriented work of the Lanyon-Phillips agency as having taken the campaign to the brink of disaster, from which it was rescued in the late stages by a shift in strategy.

Shawn Thomas, Peter Lanyon, and Chuck Phillips, while not going as far as Heaney, did share the view that the campaign had relied too heavily on evoking emotion. Said Thomas, "In hindsight, they [the TV ads] lacked substance." Lanyon reported,

> There are so many things I would do differently now. I preferred the spontaneity and authenticity of the film [*A New Journey*] to the re-shoot we ended up doing to fit the limitations of 30-second TV spots. I would have used an even more documentary look to the filming. I would have "dialed up" [increased] the information in the film. But at the time, there was no time to carefully weigh everything and make it just so.

The polling results showed that support for the Treaty fluctuated during the autumn of 1998, but that it always commanded plurality support and sometimes majority support. In all likelihood, if the government's advertising campaign had not run, that support would have eroded significantly in the face of the onslaught from the Treaty's opponents.

Perhaps the greatest impact of the advertising campaign was not felt until years later when the Campbell government that replaced the NDP held a province-wide, $3.1 million, mailed ballot referendum (April 2–May 15, 2002) on the treaty process as a whole, as per an election campaign promise.[17] That referendum was fiercely opposed by aboriginal leaders. Significantly, it generated a very low participation rate (35.8%) in response to its eight highly biased questions. Despite having declared in advance that it would be bound by the results, the Liberal government essentially ignored the referendum results in the ensuing years. It is reasonable to speculate that the NDP government's campaign of advertising, speeches, and public information about the Nisga'a Treaty in 1998 had an impact

---

17. For details, see <www.elections.bc.ca/referendum/finalresults.pdf> and Elections BC (2003, p. 8).

on the referendum results and participation rate. The NDP's 1998 campaign made a strong case for the necessity of the treaty process and demonstrated the complexity of treaty issues. It may well have "inoculated" British Columbians against the over-simplification and distortions of the referendum questions, such that the results were not a political resource that the Liberal provincial government could use to try to derail the treaty settlement process in British Columbia.

Chapter Five: Questionnaire Construction and Content

What was the nature of the polling that shaped the advertising and public information campaign described in the previous chapters? To that question we turn now.

Questionnaire Construction and Timing of Entry into the Field

As far as public opinion polling goes, what public opinion gets registered with decision makers depends, of course, upon what vehicles are used for tapping public opinion and, if polling is chosen, upon what questions questionnaire designers are willing to ask.

Doug McArthur was convinced of the need to do an advertising campaign supported by polling. Said he,

> We were painfully aware that a lot of people were of the view that the best thing to do when you get into these problems of Aboriginals was to just pretend that nothing's happening, to keep it down, or ignore it, or don't talk about it, or not have a communications strategy.... The rationale or objectives we had very much created the kinds of questions we asked.

Later, he added, "I have no time for those who say you can put complicated policy issues out there before the public without any [support]."

Who determines what is in a public opinion polling questionnaire can be very important, for the determination of content is a gatekeeping opportunity where relations of power and influence and political considerations can come to the fore. For instance, my research found federal government polling in the aboriginal affairs realm to be influenced by gatekeepers' consideration of how a particular question would look to a politically motivated person using an Access to Information request to obtain the questionnaire and the findings based on it.

In the Nisga'a Treaty case under examination here, the questionnaire construction was informed by focus groups that had been done years earlier (before the Agreement-in-Principle had been reached) and in April of 1998. Focus groups during autumn 1998 were used both to inform questionnaire construction for the surveys and to ascertain responses to the advertising campaign.

In April 1998, eight focus groups were held—in Vancouver, Prince George, Terrace, and the Fraser Valley—as negotiations on the Treaty were nearing an end.[1] During the period May 11–19, the first wave of a "baseline" provincial survey involving 900 respondents was conducted.[2] Less than two weeks after the Treaty was signed on August 4, a second wave of province-wide polling was done with 600 respondents.[3] This was just after the ad campaign started. About a month later, just after the radio ads began airing, another wave of 600 interviews was conducted.[4] During the period October 28 to November 8, 1998, while the ad campaign was in full force, interviewing was done on yet another government-commissioned poll (800 interviews), and this was followed by another wave of 700 interviews the following week, November 12–17, 1998.[5] All of these surveys were done by the Angus Reid Group, a polling firm that offered the distinct advantage of not being politically identified with the NDP. Focus groups also were conducted by Angus Reid during the advertising campaign in autumn 1998, but do not appear in the British Columbia Archives.

The archives do contain two other polls done by other firms. One was a poll (involving 800 interviews and only twelve questions of which three were about the Treaty) apparently done in mid-August, 1998 by the NDP party's pollster, Viewpoints Research, for the government caucus.[6] The other was done September 22–30, 1998 by McIntyre and Mustel Research Associates for the Nisga'a Treaty Implementation Project team.[7] This latter one involved one-on-one interviews with 150 residents and focused entirely on their reactions to the radio advertisements that began airing on September 15, 1998. Altogether, between April of 1998 and January of 1999, the government spent somewhere between $250,000 and $300,000 on public opinion research, according to John Heaney, who was in a position to know.

The questionnaire construction process was highly collegial, mutually respectful, and rather calm. When asked by this researcher, no one reported either the existence of significant tensions among those involved or the veto of any proposed question. Although one interviewee contended to me that it would be unethical to use public funds "to just replicate opponents' arguments in our questions," much of that was clearly done, especially in the September questionnaire. I was told also that there was no sense of "You can't ask that!" concerning any proposed questions.

Doug McArthur noted that viewing questionnaire construction as involving the exercise of veto power over a proposed item on the questionnaire does not address their process in a very worthwhile way. He emphasized that government essentially works in teams, such that the more important question is "Who had significant influence in the construction of the questionnaire?" In that regard, and in addition to himself, he listed John Heaney, Ian Reid, Daniel Savas, and Shawn

1. BC Archives (BCA), GR-2964, Box 17, File 16, Report of April 28, 1998.
2. BCA, GR-2964, Box 17, File 17, Report of May 26, 1998.
3. BCA, GR-2964, Box 17, File 19 and 20, including Report of August 26, 1998.
4. BCA, GR-2964, Box 17, File 21, Report of September 24, 1998.
5. BCA, GR-2964, Box 17, File 23, Reports of November 10 and 18, 1998.
6. BCA, GR-2964, Box 17, File 18, Report of August 17, 1998.
7. BCA, GR-2964, Box 17, File 22, Report of September 1998.

Thomas. Furthermore, the Premier had strong views that were taken into consideration and that shaped how McArthur himself thought about the matter. Ian Reid reported that he also consulted with the Nisga'a Treaty negotiating team and with certain staff in the Ministry of Aboriginal Affairs.

One norm informing questionnaire content was that a question on political party affiliation or general election voting intention must not be asked. Said the polling firm representative, Daniel Savas, "Strangely enough, in this instance there was never a hint of 'Could you ask the political [partisanship] questions and not report them?' They could get their party pollsters to use our questionnaire." Significantly, though, in its quarterly omnibus survey Savas's firm did ask the party affiliation question and did include a key question on the Nisga'a Treaty that was also on the questionnaire for the government survey.

The highly iterative process of questionnaire construction began with Savas suggesting questions to Heaney and Reid, and them suggesting some of their own, as did Thomas. As the advertising campaign progressed, Heaney and Reid became much more involved in suggesting questions. Savas saw his role as being, in part, to ensure that questions were "balanced and fair." The draft questionnaires were presented to Deputy Minister McArthur, who would sometimes suggest changes in phraseology or would question why something was phrased a particular way. Sometimes, a given questionnaire would go through two or three such iterations. The same process applied to the interview guide for focus group sessions.

Interviewees acknowledged that sometimes there would be spirited debate about the way of phrasing a particular question, especially if it appeared too strong or inflammatory. Spirited debate also occurred between the inner circle and persons from the Treaty negotiating team who were consulted. The latter sought to ensure that the questions were faithful to the content of the Treaty,[8] whereas members of the inner circle looked upon such phraseology as too legalistic and unlikely to be understood by members of the public. A huge debate erupted over the use of the term "land claims" as opposed to "treaty negotiations." On rare occasions, debates about phraseology were resolved by asking one phraseology of the question to half the sample and a slightly different phraseology to the other half of the sample.

Most of the disagreement about questionnaire content revolved around whether to continue including certain questions in subsequent pollings for purposes of tracking opinion change or stability over time (#9914292). One example of the focus of such a debate was the question on whether the respondent had discussed the Treaty with others, and, if so, whether they generally approved or disapproved of the Treaty. Said McArthur about this question,

---

8. Comments by Chief Treaty Negotiator Jack Ebbels on the topic of advertising are also applicable to polling. Said he, "All the treaty issues are quite complex and take a considerable amount of time, not to mention treaty language, to explain and are not that amenable to sound bites. Summarizing provisions or issues could be quite inaccurate or miss really important stuff, not intentionally.... It's almost impossible to avoid."

> Every number you generate in polling or anything else of that sort starts to create its own significance and importance. It's there, and it gets to be treated as of some importance. There was a real question about how significant it really was or whether it was misleading us and causing us to draw invalid conclusions.

Significantly, Savas's firm was also doing the polling and focus groups for the federal government on the Nisga'a Treaty. However, relations between the province and the federal government were very strained on the Nisga'a Treaty, and Savas worked in isolation from what his colleagues were doing for the federal government.

Questionnaire Content: "McArthur Was Not About to Swallow Happy Talk"

Conducting a so-called "cooked" poll—one that uses biased questions in order to obtain the client's preferred results that can then be leaked or released to the mass media—is not unknown in the polling industry.[9] Doug McArthur and his colleagues knew precisely what they wanted from the polling. As McArthur recounted, they had to find out the direction (supportive or unsupportive) of public opinion, its trend over time, why support was changing (if it was), where the weaknesses were in the support for the Treaty (what kinds of things were causing people concern), and what kinds of arguments worked to explain and gain support for the Treaty. Given that clear focus by persons who were quite experienced at polling, and given that they would not be releasing the polling results to the media, they had no use for polling questions designed to produce a predetermined outcome. As pollster Daniel Savas said, "McArthur was not about to swallow happy talk." This section will examine what did make it onto the polling questionnaires, beginning with the August 1998 questionnaire. Appendix 6 summarizes the content of that questionnaire and of one that went into the field in September 1998, just after the beginning of the radio ad campaign. They are juxtaposed for ease of comparison.[10]

The August 1998 questionnaire used in assessing public opinion surrounding the Nisga'a settlement and media campaign was of fairly standard design, for, as Daniel Savas noted, "We had some tried and true methods and some tried and true questions." The first question in the August questionnaire was the so-called "top of mind" question, which asked what current issue in the news respondents felt was most important and next most important. Awareness (yes v. no) of the Nisga'a

---

9. One of the high profile opponents of the treaties did seek to launch a poll that would try to show that British Columbians regarded the treaties as fundamentally unjust. While "cooked" polls are probably fairly rare, examples were brought to my attention in my broader research project on polling in Ottawa and Australia. Similarly, Jacobs and Shapiro (1995/96) found the Nixon White House to be actively engaged in trying to cook polls.

10. The questionnaires themselves are available from the British Columbia Archives, GR-2964, Box 17, Files 19 and 21.

Treaty was assessed next, after which respondents who were aware of the Treaty were asked to identify what they felt were the best and worst features of the Treaty settlement. The fifth question asked all respondents whether they felt that the Treaty was a step in the right or wrong direction. Then came the question (Q5A) asking for respondents' overall assessment of the Treaty. (Did they support or oppose it?) The potential of the respondent to be politically mobilized in support of or in opposition to the Treaty was assessed next, first in terms of how likely she/he would be to join a campaign of letter writing to a newspaper or MLA and then in terms of whether the respondent had ever discussed the Treaty's content or the treaty-making process with others (friends, family, neighbours, co-workers).

After asking whether those with whom the respondent had discussed the Treaty approved or disapproved of the agreement, the questionnaire turned to asking (Q10) whether the respondent recalled reading, seeing, or hearing anything about the Treaty in any of seven different types of source.[11] Next was a question asking whether the respondent preferred to rely on the opinions of others in forming his or her own opinion about the Treaty or to reach his or her own opinion independently of what others think. Then came a question (Q12) asking about the importance to the respondent of each of ten different information sources.[12] For each source identified by the respondent as important, a follow-up probe ("Who specifically would you like to hear from?") was made.

Questions on ratification were next, first in terms of whether non-ratification would be a good or bad thing and then in terms of what would be the biggest risks of not ratifying the Treaty. On the "other side of the coin," respondents were next asked what would be the biggest benefit of ratifying the Treaty.

Next, approaching the end of the interview, respondents were asked again (Q17) whether they support or oppose the Treaty and whether strongly or moderately. This was designed to identify so-called "movers"—people who had changed their view of the Treaty since being asked essentially the same question early in the interview (Q5A). Then respondents were asked how likely they would be to change their mind over the next few months "and end up supporting [opposing] the Treaty." The final two substantive questions asked whether the signed Treaty should be put to a referendum of all British Columbians, and, if it were not put to a referendum, whether that would make the respondent more likely to support or oppose the Treaty. The questionnaire concluded with socio-demographic questions that tapped respondents' age, education, labour union membership by anyone in the household and whether such membership was in a private sector or a public sector union, aboriginal identity, and household income before taxes.

---

11. The sources listed in Q10 are television news, newspapers, magazines, radio news, radio hotline shows, radio advertising, and pamphlets.

12. The sources listed in Q12 are the federal government, the provincial government, BC opposition parties, federal opposition parties, media personalities, Nisga'a leaders, the Nisga'a people, "your own provincial MLA or MP," "people likely to be affected by the Treaty, such as business people," and "people concerned about aboriginal issues, such as church or human rights leaders."

On the basis of poll results and the political dynamic in the province, the September polling done by the Angus Reid Group retained fourteen questions in their August form, slightly changed five questions, dropped ten questions, and most significantly, added 43(!) questions, as we observe in Appendix 6. The added questions dealt with the following:

- various aspects of a free vote on the Treaty in the legislature;
- reasons respondents oppose or favour having a province-wide referendum on the Treaty;
- various other opinions about a referendum on the Treaty;
- views on the Nisga'a Treaty and treaty negotiations more generally;
- whether additional, specific pieces of information related to those views on the Nisga'a Treaty made respondents feel better or worse about that Treaty;
- the reasonableness of the dollar value of the Treaty and whether additional specific pieces of information related to the financial aspects of the Treaty made those who felt the total dollar value of the Treaty was unreasonable feel any more comfortable with the Treaty;
- general summary arguments about the Treaty; and
- the direction in which those undecided about their support or opposition for the Treaty are leaning.

It is clear that these two questionnaires are constructed with the intention of informing the advertising campaign. For instance, August's question 3, which asks what the best thing about the Treaty is, identifies a positive touchstone for future ads to mention, while the subsequent question about the worst feature of the Treaty tells the advertiser that if this perception is held by the target audience for the ads, it should be countered. September's question 10 asking about recollection of encountering the Nisga'a Treaty newspaper advertising is clearly designed to serve as an indicator of the readership penetration of the government's ads. Questions 12 and 13 in August, dealing with the importance of different sources of information on the Treaty and the specific types of person from whom the respondent would like to hear about the Treaty, are of obvious relevance to the decision as to whom to feature as a spokesperson on behalf of the Treaty in the government's advertisements. Polling results on September's question 26, which focuses on arguments that were being made by the Treaty's opponents, show which of those arguments are resonating with the public and therefore need to be countered, and which can be safely ignored. For instance, cross-tabulations might show that a particular argument of the Opposition can be ignored because it resonates only with the hardcore opponents whose views the government knew it could never change. September's questions 27 ("Suppose you knew that … ; would this make you feel better or worse about the Nisga'a Treaty?") and 29 ("Does each of the following make you any more or less concerned about the amount of money agreed upon in the Treaty?") test specific content of ads, including specific radio ads found in Box 4.2 and specific newspaper ads in the "The Nisga'a Treaty: What Does It Mean To Me?" series. The "split half" approach used in question 29i is a classic methodology used to test which variant of a communication message elicits more favourable reaction.

It is also clear that these two questionnaires are formulated with the intention of advancing the government's political objectives. August's question about the respondent's likelihood of participating in an oppositional letter-writing campaign bespeaks a clear political anxiety about opinion "activists" or "opinion leaders" and, with the help of cross-tabulations, helps the politicians identify where their political enemies are situated geographically and in the social structure. The various parts of September's question 24, pertaining to whether a referendum should be held, not only address one of the higher profile political issues associated with the entire Nisga'a ratification process, but also provide feedback on which ammunition would be most effective for NDP politicians to use in combating their political opponents. In addition, August's questions 24 and 25, about labour union membership in the respondent's household, enable the NDP to gain a sense of how its traditional political allies, labour unionists, are aligned on the issue.

The September 22–30 survey by McIntyre and Mustel was unabashedly about determining British Columbians' responses to the radio ads. Each ad was played to, and evaluated by, fifty respondents. The questionnaire of course contained a question on the respondent's degree of support for the Treaty, before and after hearing the ads. After each ad was played for the respondent, she/he was asked in an open-ended question for an "overall reaction" to it. Respondents were then asked to rate the ad on ten-point scales measuring how compelling, believable, accurate, useful, and easy to understand it is. Another open-ended question next asked what the respondent's reaction would be to including the phrase "The Nisga'a Treaty, think about it" as part of the tag line at the end of the commercials. Another asked whether anything in the ads had an impact on the respondent's opinions of the Treaty, and if so, what in particular had that impact. Three socio-demographic questions were also included.

The TV ads were subjected to focus group testing and possibly to some "mall intercepts." A survey similar to that conducted by McIntyre and Mustel was not done to gauge the nuanced reactions to the television commercials, because changing television ads is a much more expensive and more complicated matter than is changing radio ads.

Conclusion

Like the advertising and public information campaign it was designed to inform, the polling endeavour was no "two bit" operation. Its thoroughness, in terms of frequency of surveys and in terms of the depth of questioning, made it expensive. It was multifaceted, in terms of types of data collection—standard telephone interviews, plus specialized interviewing involving the playing of radio ads—and it was complemented by focus groups. It had a decidedly political component to it and had input from the very top of the BC government. It was closely orchestrated with the advertising campaign and had input from the leader of the advertising campaign. We turn now to a consideration of what it yielded.

Chapter Six: The Polling Results and Their Use

[P]ublic opinion gets its form from the social framework in which it moves, and from the social processes in play in that framework. (Blumer, 1948, quoted in Herbst, 1998, p. 13)

Results

A brief and necessarily highly selective overview of the polling findings[1] is provided here. Differences in reporting formats (e.g., collapsing "moderately supportive" and "strongly supportive" into "supportive") and the absence of the questionnaire in some of the archived reports place limits on my ability to make generalizations about the findings.

One generalization that can be made from the polling data is that results on many of the questions fluctuated but did not change drastically over time. Of particular note is the fact that the Treaty had the support of a slight majority of British Columbians shortly after it was signed, and, although that support fluctuated slightly over time, it always surpassed opposition to the Treaty by a significant margin (e.g., 56% v. 30% in August, 48% v. 37% in September, back up to 56% v. 38% by early November, and to 59% v. 34% by mid-November). This might come as a surprise to those whose assessment of the support for the Treaty was based on listening to radio talk shows or reading the David Black chain of newspapers. In addition, those who thought that the Treaty was a step in the right direction outnumbered those who thought it was a step in the wrong direction by well over a 2:1 margin (e.g., 62% v. 28% in September and 69% v. 23% in November). Awareness of the Treaty was almost universal in the province (about 90% of British Columbians in September and 96% by mid-November), and it was widely discussed with others (about 45% in September), for it was deemed to be the second most important public issue in the province, slightly behind the fisheries and slightly ahead of the economy. By mid-November, about four-fifths of British Columbians said that they recalled seeing television advertising about the Treaty, about two thirds said that they recalled seeing newspaper advertising, and about half said they recalled hearing radio advertising.

By a margin of at least 20% (usually around 54% v. 31% throughout the polling), respondents thought that failure to ratify the Treaty would be a bad thing. There was strong support for a free vote on the Treaty in the legislature, including

---

1. Data sources are from the British Columbia Archives, GR-2964, Box 17, as follows: File 18 for August, File 21 for September, and File 23 for October and November. In this chapter, where no date is specified with a finding, it signifies that available archival records show the finding varied scarcely at all across the surveys in which the question was posed. This convention is adopted to minimize cumbersome reporting of polling results.

39% in September who thought a free vote was a "very good idea" and another 34% who thought a free vote was a "good idea." A clear majority (60% in August, 56% in September, and 66% by mid-November) was of the opinion that the Treaty should be put to a referendum of all British Columbians. A slight majority (in September 52% v. 45%) felt that holding a free vote in the legislature was a good substitute for a referendum on the Treaty. Throughout the autumn, the population was about evenly split on whether it was more important to ratify the Treaty than to have a referendum on it and on whether the government should immediately ratify the Treaty or delay ratifying it. Most of the specific arguments in favour of a referendum were explored in the September poll and resonated positively with a slight majority of the respondents.

Most of the arguments raised against the Treaty did not resonate with a majority of respondents. For instance, in September only about a third of the sample agreed with the notion that the Treaty creates a race-based government, only 41% agreed that the Treaty creates a Nisga'a government that is as powerful as a province, and 47% (although this increased to 51% in November) agreed that treaties with aboriginal peoples give them special status that is unacceptable. In contrast, respondents reacted quite positively to arguments used to refute the arguments made by the opponents of the Treaty.

Throughout the autumn, respondents were about evenly divided with regard to whether the total dollar value of the Nisga'a settlement was reasonable or unreasonable. Those who thought it unreasonable tended to respond favourably to only certain arguments designed to allay their financial concerns about the Treaty. Findings on one such argument are particularly noteworthy. This was the argument (in which the federal government had put much stock) that the uncertainty caused by unresolved land claims is stopping billions of dollars in investment and thousands of new jobs in the province. Only one third of those who saw the financial provisions of the Treaty as unreasonable were less concerned upon hearing this argument.

The summary argument that it is time now to ratify the Treaty won the support of a fluctuating proportion of British Columbians over the course of the autumn, but they were usually in the slight majority (58% in September to a low of 43% in late October and back up to 52% by mid-November). The competing argument that the parties instead should go back to the negotiating table broke into a majority position (54%) only in the late October polling. It was supported by only 39% in September and by 45% by mid-November. Persons undecided on the "overall support v. oppose" question tended to lean in favour of the Treaty, especially by the end of the lengthy and informative interview. Yet, by late October, in contrast to the pattern of earlier months, the information in the interview produced a slight erosion of support for, and a slight gain in opposition to, the Treaty. October also was the period when the "high empathy" TV ads were airing.

The September results showed that about 22% of the Treaty's supporters felt strongly (as opposed to "moderately") about their support, and 21% of the Treaty's opponents held their opposition strongly. Just as persons undecided on the

BOX 6.1
Examples of Respondents' Reactions to Radio Ads

Re: "Vote/Referendum" Ad
- "Dull and boring. It sounds like it could be an ad for drunk driving or buying BC bonds. The voice was not emphatic enough. [P] It's so pointless and redundant. The message doesn't mean much to greater Vancouver residents. The people who are concerned about the Treaty are the Nisga'a people and the white people living in that region of BC. A woman's voice might be better for the ad." (p. 1)

Re: "Private Property" Ad
- "More lies. [P] I just don't believe anything they tell me."(p. 3)

Re: "Cost" Ad
- "Why does a special group of people get money? [P] I'm German. I get no money." (p. 6)

Re: "Special Status" Ad
- "I sense they're selling the Treaty. [P] One-sided, not balanced. [P] Not enough information. [P] Defensive. [P] The win's for them, but not for us. [P] They are selling it again." (p. 10.)

Re: "Break 1" Ad (not included in the campaign)
- "Good grief. Who is the idiot who came up with these tapes? [P] These are absolutely ridiculous and redundant. No wonder everyone feels our tax money is going down the drain. [P] They give you very little specific information. It tells me nothing more than what I already knew before listening to them." (p. 16)

Re: "Free Vote" Ad
- "It doesn't give me any information other than the voting. [P] The soft music and birds make me think I am getting an environmentalist message. [P] Nothing." (p. 18)
- "I liked it. [P] I like the sound effects in the background. It made it soothing. I like that he was explaining what we had to do to get the Treaty." (p. 19)

Re: "Taxpayers' Cost" Ad
- "It's just bullshit. [P] As long as they are continuing with the Treaty, it will be a loss to us all." (p. 23)

Note: "[P]" denotes the fact that the quotation following is in response to a probe by the interviewer.

Source: McIntyre & Mustel Research Associates Ltd., "Public Response to Nisga'a Treaty Radio Commercials September, 1998," BC Archives, GR 2964, Box 17, File 22.

question that tapped overall support for the Treaty were asked in which direction they were leaning, those who were supportive (whether "strongly" or "moderately") of the Treaty or opposed ("strongly" or "moderately") to it were asked how likely they were to change (the direction of) their opinion in the coming months. Those respondents' self-assessed likelihood of changing their mind on the Treaty revealed that more were likely to move in an oppositional direction than in a supportive direction. About 10% of the sample described itself as likely to move from opposition to support, but about 19% described itself as likely to move from support to opposition, for a net gain of almost 9% for those opposing the Treaty. That over a quarter of respondents were likely to change their opinion attests to the complexity of the issue and the strong and conflicting keynoting by opinion leaders.

In September, "hardcore supporters"[2] outnumbered "hardcore opponents"[3] by a margin of 23% to 17% of the total sample.

Overall, the results showed that British Columbians favoured the Treaty but that a large (sometimes very large) minority opposed it. Few were fence sitters, but potential instability of opinion was substantial. Opinions were either very nuanced or somewhat inchoate.

The McIntyre and Mustel polling on reactions to the radio ads produced not only quantitative results but also qualitative reactions to each ad. The quantitative data, of course, provided basic background demographic information and the respondent's degree of opposition to, or support for, the Treaty. Quantitative data also yielded scores for each ad on five different ten-point scales called "easy to understand," "compelling," "believable," "misinformation," and "not useful." The verbatim reactions were compiled in an appendix to the report and provided great insight into how the radio ads were being received and interpreted. Examples of comments on different ads, as contained in the verbatim quotations in the McIntyre and Mustel report, are found in Box 6.1.

Use

How were these data used? Although at times the data were shared with Cabinet and caucus, whose members were very uneasy with the Premier's strategy of creating such a high profile for the issue, the primary use of the data was to inform the advertising and public information campaigns that the government was conducting. At one level, the data were used to confirm some of McArthur's *a priori* expectations, particularly his expectation that support for the Treaty would erode after the August signing ceremony. Data on this point were used to help decide whether more emphasis should be put on communication about the Treaty. In that

---

2. Reference here is to the 38% of the total number of supporters who described themselves as "very unlikely" to overturn their support for the Treaty.

3. Reference here is to the 46% of the total number of opponents who described themselves as "very unlikely" to overturn their opposition to the Treaty.

regard, special attention was also devoted to the so-called "movers"—those who changed their opinion on the Treaty over the course of the interview.

The advertising campaign, especially the radio and print components of it, was very poll driven. Indeed, the advertising campaign was essentially the *raison d'être* of the polling campaign, and Shawn Thomas made heavy use of polling results in directing the radio and print campaign. (As noted earlier, it would have been too expensive to adapt the television campaign to the polling results in any major way. Furthermore, as one participant observed, "[the] TV was done early in campaign before things heated up.") Thomas was involved in the construction of the polling questionnaires and regarded one of his own strengths as being the ability to identify the type of information needed to determine if the ads were being successful. Asked if he saw the actual poll data, he replied, "Yes, anything I wanted to see, the minute it was ready." He also said that he probably asked for cross-tabulations from the data collection firm. Such cross-tabulations, of course, permit the analyst to identify how a particular sector of the population (e.g., blue collar workers in the BC interior) is reacting to the campaign.

The public opinion polling and focus group data were used to determine the efficacy of different messages and of different formats for communicating messages, both in the advertising campaign and in the hundreds of public information outreach meetings that the government was also holding around the province. So, for instance, the data were used to brief outreach workers before those "town hall" meetings. The data were also used for decision making about the targeting and non-targeting of advertising messages. For instance, it was discovered through the public opinion research that the opponents' message criticizing the Treaty as "race-based government" had little credibility (in inner circle lingo, "traction"), except among respondents whom the inner circle dismissed as racist. Therefore, recognizing that they would never change the opinions of those "racists," they decided not to devote more resources to trying to counter that argument, which appealed to such a narrow segment of the mass public.

The polling was also used to inform decision making on the communications campaign in other ways. Those ways included changing some of the advertisements, "dramatically" increasing the frequency of some of the ads, and determining where some ads would be placed. One of the most important decisions informed by polling results was the decision, taken late in the project, to add to the television campaign the two "rolling supers" ads that had very low production values and very low cost of production, but high informational content. John Heaney—a proponent of ads that had low production values, that appealed to British Columbians' self-interest, and that targeted persons with fiscal concerns—credits these ads with having restored forward momentum to a stalled campaign to win the public opinion battle. Heaney used polling results to back his argument that ads with such low production values were needed.

Yet, the polling results did not reign supreme. For instance, on one occasion, a decision on the communications campaign flew in the face of the polling results. That was the decision to use the Premier in radio ads.

Although different members of the inner circle held different biases about the utility of focus groups,[4] the focus groups generally were appreciated for the insights that they provided on the way in which the advertising messages were being received or would be received. The focus groups had other unanticipated effects. For instance, they revealed to McArthur what he described as "the hunger and interest people had for information on the Nisga'a Treaty." He added,

> They saw government as a good source of information, which kinda surprised me…. [Furthermore, the focus groups showed me that] no matter how much effort we put into communicating, it takes a long time for large numbers of people to absorb it.

Most interviewees were adamant that polling did not affect the content of the Agreement-in-Principle or of the Treaty. For instance, Chief Negotiator Jack Ebbels reported that, to his knowledge, there were no changes in the negotiating mandate due to polling results.[5] Of course, most of the polling was done after the Treaty had been signed. Some interviewees also professed the view that policy is too important to be determined by polling. In that regard, it is noteworthy that the public opinion data clearly favoured a province-wide referendum on the Treaty, but the NDP government refused to bow to that opinion.

One interviewee (#14251) familiar with the negotiations pointed out that the negotiators saw little value in province-wide polling on general issues, for they were much more interested in public opinion on more detailed issues and in opinion in the region of the province closest to the Treaty area. Yet, the AIP negotiators did recognize that an election (1996) was soon to come and that it was of no use to get a provision included in the AIP if that contributed to the defeat of the NDP, for a Liberal government would be far less accommodating.

Public opinion was often cited during the Treaty negotiations, mainly in the sense of emphasizing that particular outcomes would have to pass the test of public opinion. I was told that negotiators frequently took the stance that what was being proposed to them by the Nisga'a would not pass such a test of public opinion, especially when it dealt with issues having a public impact, such as the Nisga'a nation's right to exclude people from certain lands. However, the negotiating team did not commission any polling, and those assertions at the negotiating table were not based on a scientific sampling of public opinion; rather, they were just a persuasive argument. As a person familiar with the negotiations said,

---

4. Shawn Thomas reported attending many focus groups. They were supervised by Savas and usually attended by Thomas, his assistant, a representative of the advertising agency, and someone from the production staff for the TV commercials. Usually, at least five such people would be observing from behind the mirror, although sometimes several more would be present. McArthur attended one focus group session, as did Krafczyk. Heaney recalls attending only focus groups relating to strategy rather than those focussing on the ads themselves.

5. However, earlier polling might have had an impact on the NDP's decision as to what kind of an election issue the party wanted to make the Treaty in the 1996 election.

> On a daily basis I saw people's concerns and dealt face-to-face with outright opponents on a constant basis, so knew what had to be addressed and had quite a good sense of what was going to "fly" publicly and what was not going to fly. For example, I didn't need any polling to know we had to get rid of the tax exemption to make it fly publicly in BC.

Such assessments were better than mere guesswork, but in the absence of polling data and a campaign of persuasion, they might have been inadvertently misleading or even pre-emptive of public opinion. In that regard, it is significant that during the autumn of 1998, the poll results were markedly more supportive of the Treaty than one would have anticipated on the basis of exposure to the mass media.

Assessment

In conclusion, one might well ask whether the public opinion data gathered for the Nisga'a Treaty Implementation Project team actually furthered the goals of those who commissioned the data and whether the quality of the public opinion data was sufficient to support the decisions being made. Despite the fact that these particular questions were not posed to interviewees, I feel reasonably comfortable in answering them in the affirmative. There are several reasons for that comfort.

First, the members of the inner circle were seasoned political pros. One (self-assessed) strength of the director of the advertising campaign, Shawn Thomas, was knowing what kinds of questions to ask in support of an advertising campaign. Similarly, Doug McArthur's extensive experience left him with a very clear idea of precisely what objectives were to be pursued in the polling. He and Clark ensured that the financial and human resources were available to achieve those objectives, which is the second reason for my comfort. If questions needed to be included on a questionnaire or the size of the sample in a geographic region of interest needed to be increased, that was done, as was illustrated by the addition of 43 new questions to the September questionnaire and the enlargement of the sample in the northwestern part of the province. My own inspection of the questionnaire left me thinking "What more could they possibly have asked?" Thirdly, the data were provided in a timely fashion. Fourthly, as noted in the next chapter, Savas conducted intensive cross-tabular analysis ("drilling down in the data"), when so requested, in order to further specify some finding or put some possible explanation to the test. Fifthly, the Premier himself was highly engaged with the project and made it clear that it was his government's top priority. While such a commitment to the project by the Premier does not automatically ensure quality data, when combined with the other factors mentioned in this paragraph, the sense of religious zeal for the project and especially the competitive, collegial accountability that prevailed in the inner circle, it does suggest that there will be a strain toward excellence and thoroughness in the performance of those who constructed the questionnaires and performed the analyses.

The only reservation with which I should qualify my answer pertains to the team's eschewal of more sophisticated causal statistical analysis. The data might have been excellent,[6] but as we shall see in the next chapter, some explicitly causal questions were not addressed with analytical tools that could have provided causal explanations replete with appropriate statistical controls. However, for some of McArthur's and Thomas's objectives (e.g., tracking the level of support for the Treaty and the direction of changes in that support over time), this was not germane.

---

6. My research did not permit an assessment of the quality of the data in terms of such issues as sampling and interviewing quality. With regard to sampling bias arising from the use of data collection via telephone, it is worth noting that, at the time of the polling in 1998, interviewee resistance and inaccessibility were probably much lower than they are today.

Chapter Seven: Gatekeeping, Analysis, and Interpretation of the Data in the Inner Circle

Gatekeeping

The possibility of "gatekeeping," or the withholding of information, is a vital matter implicit in Blumer's call for researchers to work backwards from decision makers in the study of public opinion. It was a key concern in the present research.

As noted earlier, the Nisga'a Treaty was the main political preoccupation of the provincial government during the period under consideration. Not surprisingly, therefore, much secrecy surrounded the polling results. However, the gatekeeping that occurred within the inner circle was minor. Among those key players, there was a rather thorough airing of the data.

Deputy Minister McArthur was described by more than one interviewee as being very passionate about the Treaty and very engaged in the project. He not only was fully aware of the content of the questionnaire but demanded the full results from each evening's interviewing. He also attended one of the focus groups. His experience had led him to anticipate gatekeeping, for, as he noted, "Polling information creates power for people who have possession of it. But I was seized with that possibility and made sure it doesn't happen." He went on to point out that he received full reports and that, for tracking surveys, there is no detailed interpretive narrative provided with the quantitative data. Although executive summaries were provided, he was adamant that he'd never rely upon executive summaries as his source of information.

The Premier was more interested in public opinion survey results than are most other premiers. He personally went over in detail the results from some of the main polls, on his own, in settings other than meetings. In addition, he was not passive when being briefed; there was a lot of interaction, and he was prepared to take an aggressive stance. Furthermore, getting the Treaty ratified was his highest priority that autumn. In light of these factors, to anyone else in the inner circle who might have entertained gatekeeping tactics even fleetingly, it was clear that this would be a very high risk strategy for his own career. As a result, the Premier was able to have full confidence that his staff and officials were being forthright with him concerning the public opinion findings on the Nisga'a Treaty issue.

From the perspective of pollster Daniel Savas, gatekeeping was a non-issue. Not only was he required to provide the full quantitative results, but his personal assessment of McArthur and his colleagues militated against other forms of selectivity. Said Savas about his clients on this project, "They're very savvy people."

Did the inner circle engage in gatekeeping behaviour vis-à-vis Cabinet and caucus? Conflicting findings emerged here. McArthur, the former Saskatchewan cabinet minister, said, "We had no interest in withholding information [from caucus and Cabinet]." He went on to say that Cabinet and caucus were shown the results on the tracking questions, including the data showing the initial decline in support for the Treaty. "I can't think of any actual withholding of data from Cabinet for [the] purpose of not informing them of something you didn't want them to know," he said. Cabinet and caucus were also shown how the public opinion polling results were being used to shape the communication campaign. Another interviewee (#14291) said that the public opinion data had a "very marginally positive effect" on relations with Cabinet and caucus, "because the public opinion data was, by and large, positive." However, he added, "Cabinet was reasonably interested, but they weren't given much because Cabinet and caucus didn't agree with the strategy the Premier was pursuing. It was a selective release."

The secrecy surrounding the public opinion findings was normal for government polling on sensitive, high priority issues. Said one interviewee about releasing polling results more broadly, "It's very distracting; people get all caught up in the poll results. It's best used by professionals."

Analysis

Given that opinions on many aspects of the Treaty were relatively evenly divided, somewhat unstable, and nuanced or even inchoate, and given how much money was to be spent on advertising, one might reasonably expect a causal analysis to have been undertaken to answer the question "What is shaping public opinion on this issue?" For instance, a multiple regression analysis could have identified the relative causal weight of various independent variables in shaping support for or opposition to the Treaty, simultaneously holding constant the other independent variables in the analysis. Furthermore, for these same reasons and to target the advertising, one might reasonably expect a more refined characterization of the mass public into different segments ("segmentation analysis"), such as the Angus Reid Group did in a large national survey on aboriginal matters earlier in 1998. At the very least, one might have expected the polling firm to have produced a refined breakdown of the location in the social structure (e.g., in terms of social class position) of holders of certain opinions on the Treaty issue. However, these are not to be found in the archived reports, which rely on simple frequency distributions, cross-tabulations by region of the province, and, in one report only, chi-squared statistics with significance levels. Almost no statistical analysis of even a moderate level of sophistication was done on the data, although "reams" of cross-tabulations were done.

My research in Ottawa and Australia leads to the expectation that, in addition to formal reports, there will be a form of informal reporting of survey results. There was informal reporting on this project, but it was not of the type suggested in the previous paragraph (#1501). Ian Reid did report that segmentation analysis was conducted, although he provided no further information about it. John Heaney reported that they sometimes did some "drilling down more deeply into the cross-tabs" by asking pollster Daniel Savas to go back and do more cross-tabulations. This was done, for instance, to isolate the "movers" (those who changed their support or opposition to the Treaty from the beginning to the end of the interview) and to determine "where they're with the public and where they deviate [with regard to the arguments used by the protagonists]."

McArthur spoke to me in correlational terms when he said, "Weakness in support for this treaty was associated with th[e] process issue [that is, whether there should be a referendum]." However, when asked if he had ever asked the pollster for the strength of correlation coefficients between certain variables, he replied, "No, we didn't do much of that kind of analysis. Why? I don't know. That's a good question. We did some tabular breakdowns."

Others suggested an answer. Despite the fact that the client—namely, members of the inner circle—was described as "very savvy" and "sophisticated," that sophistication was not believed to extend to intermediate-level statistical analysis. With regard to the potential audience beyond the inner circle, Ian Reid submitted that

> Trying to explain regression to a cabinet minister is not helpful. You want to make sure your analysis will answer their questions and not raise ones you can't hope to explain in a cabinet presentation. *You need to have the data tell a coherent story as much as possible.* (emphasis not in original)

Both John Heaney and Daniel Savas pointed to the small sample size as not permitting detailed cross-tabulations. They also pointed to the time imperative: the fact that there was little time available. Indeed, the time imperative very much militated against such analysis, for as Doug McArthur said, "I made it very clear that poll results would be transmitted to me in real time—the full results from the night before by the next morning in hard copy or electronically."

Said pollster Daniel Savas,

> I can't agree with you more that it would be helpful to go beyond zero order relations to controls and causal analysis to inform the communications campaign, but we didn't do regression analysis on Nisga'a.... [Failure to do so] is a failure of the business side of polling.... [However,] clients could question the reliability of the causal relationship.

Savas's remarks are worth quoting at greater length because they provide insights into the epistemology (ways of knowing) that guided the polling and because they point to the fundamentally sociological nature of the transaction between pollster and client. Impression management by the pollster, for face-saving and other reasons, is clearly part of the sociological relationship between pollster and client. In that regard, note the implication that the pollster would face embarrassment in front of the client if the R-squared value were not large enough—that is, if he could not explain a large enough proportion of the variance in a dependent variable. What is left unspoken is the implication that the pollster would lose some of the mystique upon which his profession is based, and would also lose some of his authoritative demeanour.

> Yes, we do think about causal analysis, and yes, such analysis is done, but, with this kind of an issue and the nature of the context in which we were operating, [PAUSE] I don't know that they would want that kind of analysis. They wouldn't know what to do with it. I really got a sense that they had a gut feeling about what was going on, and they were really trying to find out to what extent [that was accurate]. Certainly, some regression analysis might have helped, but [VOICE TRAILS OFF; SENTENCE NOT COMPLETED]. Sure, we can invest some time in trying to educate the client, but what happens if, at the end of the day, your R-squared is .05? Then what do you say to the client? "I wasted a couple hours of my analyst's time, and I'm sitting there trying to figure what's going on and, by the way, why did I put those variables into the equation and not others?" Well, Geez, I don't know—cross-tabs just seem so much more straightforward. [When you rely only on cross-tabs] you're deducing a lot more, and you're using a little bit more of your intuition based on your understanding of the way things are going, but [SENTENCE NOT FINISHED]. What's your dependent variable even [going to be in a regression analysis]?

Ironically, in the minds of the clients, the legitimacy of the pollster's expertise might be compromised by the use of more sophisticated statistical methodology, as the more sophisticated statistical analysis could produce more "loose ends" or could raise more questions than the pollster can answer. Thus, the ability of the pollster to manage the relationship with the client and to justify fees to the client could be undermined.

Ian Reid's previously quoted remarks about the need to have the data "tell a coherent story as much as possible" also are highly germane here. That is, even in the non-commercial relationship between in-house analyst and cabinet minister, the analyst is loath to introduce complexities that would affect his relationship with the minister-as-client.

Interpretations

As symbolic interactionist theory emphasizes, human beings are meaning-seeking animals. Presented with a situation, we construct a *meaning* or *interpretation* to guide us in our reactions to it. Sometimes, those interpretations involve assimilating the situation to an existing frame of reference, whereas, at other times, we realign or even transform our frame of reference (Snow et al., 1986). Such meaning-seeking and significance-attributing activity was an integral part of processing the Nisga'a Treaty polling data, for collegial debate on how to interpret the findings was commonplace in the inner circle, particularly with regard to how the findings related to the communications campaign and how regional differences were to be interpreted. Said McArthur, "We'd wrestle different interpretations to the ground."

One interpretive frame upon which the inner circle seized was provided by McArthur, on the basis of his experience in Saskatchewan and Yukon. As noted in Chapter Three, that experience had created in him a concern right from the outset—namely, that support for the Treaty would erode over time as organized opposition mobilized and the issue got drawn out in the coffee shops, radio call-in shows, "op-ed" pieces, and letters to the editor. Thus, the fluctuation in support that we noted earlier was viewed among the insiders as erosion rather than as random variation or as the patterned swing of a pendulum. McArthur's *a priori* frame was consistent with the need for an aggressive and detailed public communication campaign and a polling effort to monitor and refine that public communication.[1] The most they could hope, McArthur came to believe, was that, with a successful advertising and public information campaign, they could bring support for the Treaty up to about 60%.

Seemingly different from McArthur's frame, yet consistent with it insofar as the importance of the communication campaign was concerned, was another interpretation provided by Heaney. Said he, "The majority supporting the Treaty was nascent until we actualized them with our advertising campaign."

A consensus came to prevail on several interpretations of the findings. Foremost among them was the notion that the hardcore of opposition to the Treaty was greater than the core support and had "more room to grow" than did the hardcore support. Indeed, much of the support was interpreted as "soft."

Do the data support this interpretation? Not necessarily. In Box 7.1, I put the interpretation to the test, although, admittedly, the data used for that test are from only one survey. There, the "hardcore supporters" of the Treaty were found to outnumber the "hardcore opponents" by a margin of about 6%. This contradicts the interpretation that prevailed in the inner circle.

Do the opponents have "more room to grow" than the supporters? In Box 7.1, I found that the answer is "yes," as 19.1% of the total sample comprises supporters who assess themselves as likely to become opponents, but only 10.4% of the sample comprises opponents who assess themselves as likely to become supporters—a likely net gain of 8.7% for the opponents. So, on the basis of this survey, the inner circle's interpretation that the opponents had more "room to grow" than did those in favour of the Treaty can be said to be accurate.

---

1. There is no intimation here that McArthur had a hidden agenda.

BOX 7.1
Assessing the Inner Circle's Interpretations of Support for and Opposition to the Treaty and the Growth Potential of Each

Let us consider first the notion that hardcore opposition was greater than hardcore support. The report of September 24 showed that the end-of-interview support question (Q31) yielded the following distribution of opinion:

22%	Strongly support the Treaty	(a)
36%	Moderately support	(b)
5%	Don't know	(c)
16%	Moderately oppose	(d)
21%	Strongly oppose	(e)

Those who replied "Don't know" (c) were asked Q32: "Which way are you currently leaning?" The distribution of responses to that question was as follows:

35%	Leaning toward supporting the Treaty	(f)
7%	Leaning toward opposing the Treaty	(g)

The remaining 58% (h) of those in category "c" were presumably quite undecided and not leaning in either direction.

Those (d + e + (7% of c)) who were opposed in response to Q31 or Q32 were asked Q33: "Is it likely or not likely that you could change you mind over the next few months and end up supporting the Treaty? Would that be very or somewhat likely/unlikely?" Among the 37% (= 21% + 16% + (7% of 5%)) of the sample asked this question, the response breakdown was as follows:

3%	Very likely to end up supporting the Treaty	(j)
25%	Somewhat likely to end up supporting the Treaty	(k)
25%	Somewhat unlikely to end up supporting the Treaty	(l)
46%	Very unlikely to end up supporting the Treaty	(m)

That last response category (m) can be considered to be the "hardcore opponents" of the Treaty. They constitute 17% [= 46% of 37% = (m × (d + e + (g × c)))] of the respondents in the entire sample.

In addition, those (a + b + (35% of c)) who were in favour of the Treaty in Q31 or Q32 were asked Q34: "Is it likely or not likely that you could change your mind over the next few months and end up opposing the Treaty? Would that be very or somewhat likely/unlikely?" Among the 60% (= 22% + 36% + (35% of 5%)) of the sample asked this question, the response breakdown was as follows:

4%	Very likely to end up opposing the Treaty	(n)
28%	Somewhat likely to end up opposing the Treaty	(o)
27%	Somewhat unlikely to end up opposing the Treaty	(p)
38%	Very unlikely to end up opposing the Treaty	(q)

That last response category (q) can be considered to be the "hardcore supporters" of the Treaty. They constitute 23% [= 38% of 60% = (q × (a+b+(f × c)))] of the sample. They outnumber the "hardcore opponents" by a margin of about 6%. That contradicts the interpretation that prevailed in the inner circle.

Do the opponents "have more room to grow" than the supporters? To answer this we take into account those who are likely to change their opinion, whether "somewhat" or "very likely."

How many opponents are "somewhat" or "very" likely to become supporters? The answer is 10.4% of the total sample, calculated as $(j + k) \times ((d + e) + (g \times c))$. How many supporters are likely to become opponents? The answer is 19.1% of the total sample, calculated as $(n + o) \times ((a + b) + (f \times c))$. Thus, a net gain of 8.7% of the sample can be anticipated in this manner for the opponents of the Treaty. So, the inner circle's interpretation that the opponents had more "room to grow" than did those in favour of the Treaty is accurate in this survey.

A related interpretation revolved around what polling results constituted "good news" and what constituted "bad news" (political danger for the Treaty's prospects of ratification). Said Savas, "We tried to suggest the red flags they had to pay attention to if they were going to a) get it through with public support and b) not have the province go up in arms because this thing was either rammed through or whatnot."

One of those red flags was itself contested terrain. Reference here is to the question (#8 on both the August and September surveys) that asked respondents "Have you ever discussed the Nisga'a Treaty with neighbours, friends, family, or co-workers, either in terms of its contents or the process used to arrive at it?" Its follow-up question (#9) asked those who replied in the affirmative "And would you say that THEY generally approve or disapprove of this agreement?"[2] There was some considerable discussion within the inner circle as to both whether that question was well formulated and what its findings meant, for there was a dissonance between what respondents thought their discussion partner's position was and what the earlier question that directly measured support showed. That discrepancy in findings raised the question as to whether, in the earlier question, respondents had skewed their answers about their own opinions. So, the issue became one of whether the question about how their neighbours/friends/ family/co-workers felt was actually tapping how the respondents themselves really felt. That is, was the neighbours/friends/family/co-workers question a better indicator and was it pointing to a looming shift in opinion about which the implementation team should be concerned? Angus Reid, founder of the polling firm that bears his name, personally placed great importance on this question for predicting future changes in opinion. So, in McArthur's words, "It caused us a lot of concern and we never did improve upon our ability to interpret the results of that question."

Recall that a clear majority of British Columbians held the opinion that the Treaty should be put to a province-wide referendum. Related to that was another

---

2. On the August 19, 1998 survey, 45% had discussed the Treaty with others and 59% of that 45% said that their discussion partner(s) generally disapproved of the agreement, while only 31% said that their discussion partner(s) generally approved of the agreement.

issue that was the focus of much debate within the inner circle, namely, the matter of whether people's sympathy for a referendum was somehow a concern about the *process* being undemocratic and whether or not a free vote in the legislature would be, in their view, a reasonable substitute for a referendum. This interpretive challenge in the August survey results led to the addition of eleven referendum-related questions on the September survey to resolve the interpretive debate.

Interpretations were also offered as to why people supported or opposed the Treaty. For instance, a May 26, 1998 Angus Reid Group executive summary document[3] dealt with several different questions (some of which were open ended) on a May 11–19, 1998 survey of 900 British Columbians. It reported that positive attitudes toward land claim settlements in general or the Nisga'a Treaty in particular (different questions), were based on such foundations as

- a sense of urgency to get the land claims settled (72%),
- the belief that investment was being lost because of uncertainty over land claims (61%),
- a sense that the issue had been dragging on for too long (79%),
- a belief that the Nisga'a deserve to get something for past injustices (20%) and that the Treaty is a reasonable instrument and fair to all sides (15%),
- a belief that signing land claims will reduce confrontations and protests (61%), and
- a belief that the Treaty eliminates "special status" for the Nisga'a (no data given, other than the finding that 86% strongly support the fact that the Nisga'a will be subject to Canadian and BC laws).

Opposition to the Treaty or to land claims settlement was traced in the report to these beliefs:

- land claims are too important to rush (63%),
- today's generations are not responsible for past mistakes or injustices (60%),
- the Nisga'a are asking for too much (24%) or the deal is too generous (11%),
- the Treaty offers no finality (12%),
- the Nisga'a have been given enough already (11%), or
- everyone should be treated equally (11%).

This was summarized as follows: "[W]hat is likely driving opposition to signing the treaty is a resistance to the land and financial compensation components of the agreement."

---

3. "BC Ministry of Aboriginal Affairs—Nisga'a Survey—Executive Summary," BC Archives, Call No. GR2964, Box 17, File 17.

Savas picked up on respondents' contradictory readings of the Treaty as both eliminating and reinforcing "special status" for the Nisga'a. He commented,

> If you can sell the Nisga'a Treaty in terms of eliminating that special treatment, it would help[4] because that was the real driving fact behind this. The political culture in this province is really driven by treating everyone the same—no special status, no special rights, that kind of stuff.

Interestingly, though, the fact that 86% of respondents strongly supported the "no special status" feature of the Nisga'a Treaty suggests that this factor is practically a constant, rather than a variable. Ordinarily, a *constant* cannot explain variation in a dependent *variable*, but Savas's interpretation seeks to circumvent that. Yet, his comment fails to take into account that only 11% of British Columbians gave "everyone should be treated equally" as a reason for opposing the Nisga'a Treaty. The point here is that the official report on the survey results is laden with interpretation that the executive summary reader is asked to take at face value, even though a statistically more sophisticated reader would have questions about the analysis and would probably want to see a regression analysis[5] before feeling comfortable with statements about what is "driving" support for or opposition to the Treaty.

Handling Nuance

Ambiguity, contradiction, and nuance are often integral aspects of public opinion on political issues. Some pollsters are of the firm belief that simplification is part of their job in reporting to their client. Hence, nuances of public opinion tend to get obscured. As an executive in the national office of a polling firm told me during the larger study, "I can't say, 'On the one hand ..., and on the other hand ... and my foot says ...' Yes, contradictions do get weeded out, but you live or die by the quality of your advice."

In contrast, the inner circle in Victoria embraced nuance. The remarks of pollster Daniel Savas again bear quoting at length:

> Definitely, I gave them the nuances if there was ambiguity or contradiction in the results, for a couple of reasons: a) that's our job and b) they would see them anyway. Presenting them [the client] with all of the nuances was an important part of the relationship with the client and of the reporting. They were looking to us for nuances....

---

4. Note that the "It's not about politics" ad attempted to do precisely that through its inclusion of reference to the Nisga'a as sacrificing "their personal tax exempt status to achieve that dream and take their place as equals in Canadian society."

5. Regression analysis offers the attraction of being able to assess the respective weight of each of numerous independent variables in shaping an outcome (such as support for the Treaty), while simultaneously controlling for all of the independent variables in the analysis.

I think they valued our abilities to give them nuance, remembering of course, that this isn't an exact science. You know, one attitudinal statement or two doesn't necessarily produce exact results. There's a lot of grey area.... Aboriginal issues touch some basic core values of people, be it equality, justice, [or] tolerance. You push any one of those "buttons," and there's a risk. And so, the nuance was important. The grey areas around the results were as important as the non-grey areas because it would give some sense in terms of what might happen and what buttons might be pushed, based on the nuance. So, we *had* to do that.... At the end of the day, public opinion *is nuance*; public opinion research is nuance research.... So, in many ways, I think the nuance is more important. And in this particular instance, I think it was critical, because they had to have an understanding of what the "red flags" [were] and what the potential for risk [was] in terms of going one way or the other. You've got the potential for it to become really, really explosive and out of hand for them, and they were very conscious of that, I think anyway.

John Heaney reinforced this view when he spoke of the fact that ambiguity, contradiction, and caveat were not eliminated from his reports because "we work for sophisticated people." He added, "Communicating caveat is an important part of our job, especially for those who want to make findings actionable as is." Ian Reid concurred wholeheartedly. His reference to avoiding creating "a hot button" reinforces Savas's point about "buttons" and underscores a conceptualization of public opinion research as risk aversion activity:

I think it's important to let it come out. A lot of it is rooted in the phraseology of the question. It's important not to paper them over. If it's a key area, for example, special status or fisheries, the audience should know how it works [with some of its nuances]. We try to explore below the surface of contradictions on key issues. If I don't understand how it works, I could be advising someone to go down a really bad road. Contradiction tells us where we have to do more work. It can be helpful in enabling us to avoid creating a hot button in our communications.

Sometimes, contradictions in the data were interpreted positively. Heaney recalled suggesting that the team should not get depressed by a particular result, because it was somewhat mitigated by another finding.

Nuance was handled differently for different audiences. For instance, in contrast to the rich detail he presented to McArthur and the Premier, with other audiences one interviewee would concentrate on data that "fit" a "story." In his words,

The best way to brief people is to tell a story that makes sense to them. I look at what my audience is—their interest, who they deal with that make life difficult for them, etc. For instance, negotiators work with knowledgeable stakeholders, whereas MLAs work with people with little information. There are some very basic patterns in opinion on aboriginal issues in BC that have not changed in a long time—for instance, the proportion of the population falling in each segment. Much of my story is how things don't change even though the debate is very volatile.

That approach is essentially one of developing a mini-theory of public opinion in the policy area. Interestingly, an interviewee (#990912) involved in the federal government's Nisga'a polling pointed to certain dangers associated with that approach. Said he,

Pollsters tend to become known for, and I think tend to believe, that public opinion in a certain [policy] sector works a certain way. I think sometimes it's hard for people to adjust their thinking, even in the presence of new data or new findings. What I really try to do is avoid becoming so firm in one worldview that I cannot react to new data. I don't want to own a theory about aboriginal public opinion, because I think it becomes hard to change your view. So I'm always on guard for that; if something new pops up, let's make sure we acknowledge it; don't try to bury it. That's certainly what some pollsters will do. I don't have an agenda; I think that's very important.

Nuance is detail. Some questionnaires offer more detail than others, and some forums for communicating polling results admit of more detail than others, just as some audiences desire and can "digest" more detail than others. In the processing of the Nisga'a Treaty polling data within the BC government, nuance was indulged. After all, not only were the principal players fully accustomed to creating and working with polling data, but most were quite accustomed to dealing with polling data on aboriginal issues, per se. Furthermore, during the period under study here, the issue was the major preoccupation of the Premier, his Deputy Minister, the government, and the Opposition. The political stakes were very high, and massive human and fiscal resources were being devoted to the Nisga'a project. The Premier himself was a main catalyst for the idea of intensive polling and tracking being done at all. He was involved in shaping the questionnaire content, was briefed regularly and at length on findings, kept abreast of tracking results, studied the printouts on his own, and needed to be familiar with some of the nuance in order to be able to hold sway in a caucus and Cabinet that were uneasy with the high budget, high profile approach that the Party and the government were taking on the issue. All of these factors point to an atypical situation, when compared to the situation surrounding most issues that become the focus of government polling. Therefore, it is not surprising that nuance would be admitted, even cultivated, in this situation but not in others.

Conclusion

The present consideration of the analysis and interpretation of the findings suggests a paradoxical mix of raw power tempered by the collegial, team-based organizational environment that Campbell and Szablowski's (1979) portrayal of the "super-bureaucrats" would lead us to expect. The Premier and his Deputy Minister had the power and were not hesitant about using it: Glenn Clark would brook no significant opposition on the Nisga'a issue within the team or the party, while Doug McArthur acted decisively to structure the situation in such a way as to ensure that he was not the victim of gatekeeping by others. In some important ways, both men took a very "hands-on" approach to the file, although Clark clearly delegated responsibility for day-to-day management of the polling, advertising, and public information campaign to McArthur.

Beyond the team, secrecy enveloped the findings, but findings were shared widely within the team. That is consistent with the collegial model mentioned above. Similarly, debate over the meaning of findings was permitted in the inner circle meetings,[6] for these men were seasoned professionals with much political and polling experience from which to draw their interpretations of the data and its practical significance for the campaign.

Statistical weapons were not fully deployed in this political battle. There were several reasons for this, including time constraints and the very pragmatic issues of targeting messages for segments of the political market who could be identified through the use of simple statistical techniques. Another important reason to emerge here, though, is that to deconstruct the data statistically might also be to deconstruct the mystique and specialized authority of those who have a vested interest in maintaining that mystique and authority—particularly professional pollsters. Similarly, their relationship with the client could be jeopardized by the sometimes less than "tidy" results produced by advanced statistical analysis.[7] Furthermore, in situations such as this, pollsters and advertising "gurus" turn to trusted methodologies. A high stakes political issue driven by a desperate government operating under tight time constraints is not a setting conducive to such actors "thinking outside the box" of conventional questions and conventional analytic techniques.

Certain interpretations of the data came to be normative within the team, although at least one of them was found here to be inaccurate in at least one of

---

6. The reader may recall that the Premier did not attend these meetings.

7. For instance, to report that you have explained 40% of the variance in a dependent variable is to admit to the client that, for the most part, you don't know what's "going on" causally in the relationships between dependent and independent variables. Conversely, in academic social science circles, explaining 40% of the variance is usually quite a respectable outcome.

the surveys. Earlier public opinion writing by Blumer and by Turner and Killian (1987, pp. 159–161) emphasized the emergent normative properties of public opinion in the mass public. Findings in the present study suggest that the emergent norm phenomenon can also operate within the inner sanctum of the political elite. That is to say, peer pressure to conform to prevailing interpretations can operate even in the lofty reaches of government.

Consistent with the notion that a major reason for polling is to reduce political risk, I found that interviewees frequently spoke about "red flags" and the need to avoid "hot buttons." Such concerns were an important lens through which members of the inner circle interpreted the polling data. The same concerns helped shape the questionnaire in the earlier phase of the project.

Where interpretive ambiguity arose, the members of the inner circle had the luxury of being able to "throw more resources" at the problem, as illustrated by the addition of eleven questions about a referendum to the questionnaire for the September survey.

An important part of the analysis was the identification of which arguments were effective at eliciting support for the Treaty, and which were not. Under the circumstances, this focus is hardly remarkable. Significantly, though, when coupled with some simple statistical cross-tabulations, the emphasis on mobilizing support for the Treaty led to the dismissal of some types of British Columbians as "racists" and to the abandonment of attempts to influence their opinions in the advertising campaign.

Finally, for the sophisticated men who comprised the inner circle, nuance was embraced, not eschewed. Although interviews did not explore this, it is conceivable that the handling of nuance served to provide a forum for the playing out of the competitive collegial accountability about which Campbell and Szablowski (1979, p. 188) wrote in describing the "super-bureaucrats." (See Box 1.2.)

Chapter Eight: Processing Public Opinion on Reconciliation in Australia

In this chapter, I place the British Columbia case study in a comparative, international context by examining the processing of public opinion on Indigenous issues in Australia. The Australian case study used is that involving the official reconciliation process there. It was led by the Council for Aboriginal Reconciliation (CAR), an independent body that was appointed by the Commonwealth (federal) government. My Australian research, like the Canadian, was driven by the desire to understand public opinion, as Herbert Blumer advocated, "from the other end." The purpose of this case study is to expand the basis for making generalizations about how elite political actors process public opinion data on Indigenous[1] issues.

The Australian Context

> If the Government's vision of justice is restricted to one that is relevant to itself, I despair for my country and regret the ignorance of political leaders who do not appreciate what is required to achieve true reconciliation for us as a nation."
> (From the letter of resignation of CAR Chairman, Patrick Dodson, to Minister for Aboriginal Affairs, October 30, 1997, quoted in Kingston [1997a])

Generally speaking, Indigenous issues usually have been of lesser political salience at the national level in Australia than in Canada. Admittedly, at the state level in Australia, Indigenous issues have, on occasion, been profitably exploited by politicians. For instance, the government of Western Australia has been accused of "playing the Aboriginal card" when in political trouble. However, having found in interviews in two different states—Queensland and Western Australia—that state government polling on Indigenous issues is extremely rare, I chose for the Australian case study an Indigenous issue in which the Commonwealth government was the primary political actor. As mentioned, that issue is reconciliation between Indigenous Australians and the larger Australian society as represented by the Commonwealth government.

According to a veteran Australian pollster (interviewee #1611), public interest in controversial Indigenous issues tends to be intense, but extremely short-lived.

---

1. In this chapter, we use the term "Indigenous" instead of "aboriginal," except when quoting others or referring to proper nouns. The term "Indigenous" encompasses both Aborigines and Torres Strait Islanders.

For instance, even in response to the Australian High Court's original 1992 land-mark decision in the highly consequential *Mabo* case on Native title, polls showed a peaking of interest described by the pollster as "not even a tooth—more like a stalagmite", and then the issue disappeared. That same pollster said that my description of public opinion on aboriginal issues in Canada is "one hundred per cent" applicable to Australia—namely, that awareness of Indigenous issues and the importance attached to those issues are both extremely low in the mass public unless the Pope of the Roman Catholic Church is involved or the issue affects the person's livelihood or otherwise directly touches the person's own life. Indeed, at the Commonwealth level in Australia, the *Realpolitik* sometimes appears to be one of getting Indigenous issues "out of the way" as quickly as possible because they distract from other issues that the government deems to be more important.

Much polling on Indigenous issues is done in Australia, but it is usually done by media conglomerates rather than governments. The reconciliation issue was a noteworthy exception in which the Council for Aboriginal Reconciliation was actively involved in both extensive polling and focus group research dating back to 1991. The focus in this chapter will be on the period in late 1999 and early 2000 when both quantitative (survey) and qualitative (focus group) soundings of public opinion were taken in preparation for the final report of the Council for Aboriginal Reconciliation.

A major difference between the British Columbian and Australian case studies is in the orientation of the respective First Ministers, Premier Glen Clark and Prime Minister John Howard. Whereas the Treaty was the Clark government's highest priority during the period under study, in Australia, Howard had already repeatedly asserted his steadfast opposition to a cornerstone of the reconciliation process—a Commonwealth government apology to the Indigenous people of Australia. Indeed, as the above quotation from Patrick Dodson suggests, in the late 1990s and beyond, relations between the Howard government and the Council were so poor as to be antagonistic.

However, Howard had "inherited" the Council for Aboriginal Reconciliation (CAR), which was created by Parliament under the Labor government by means of the *Council for Aboriginal Reconciliation Act, 1991.*[2] It passed unanimously in both houses of the Commonwealth Parliament.[3] The statute gave the Council the mandate of promoting a process of reconciliation between Aboriginal and Torres

---

2. Inasmuch as John Howard had been a key member of the Opposition with whom then-Prime Minister Hawke had negotiated all-party support for the CAR Act in 1991, when Howard became Prime Minister he could not have readily disavowed the Council, if he had so desired.

3. Much of the information in this paragraph is taken from the Department of the Prime Minister and Cabinet (1999), as provided by Senator John Faulkner, Leader of the Opposition in the Senate. I am grateful to Senator Faulkner, who gave me access to all 154 documents he received in response to his Freedom of Information request for "all documents held by the Department of the Prime Minister's Office relating to the commissioning, conduct, format and results of qualitative and/or quantitative public opinion research undertaken by or for the Council for Aboriginal Reconciliation since 1 July 1999."

Strait Islander peoples and the wider community, with the aim of achieving definite outcomes by January 1, 2001 (the centenary of the federation), at which time the Council would go out of existence. Parliament specifically asked the Council to report on whether a document or documents of reconciliation would advance the process, and, if so, to make recommendations on the form and content of such documents. It was such a document, or declaration toward reconciliation, that was a key focus of the polling and focus groups in the present case study. (See Appendix 11 and Appendix 12 for the draft and the final reconciliation declarations.)

The twenty-five member Council had fourteen Indigenous members, including two Torres Strait Islanders. Nine were drawn from the wider Australian community, including appointees from the three main political parties. The Council's secretariat of approximately twenty persons was housed in the Reconciliation and Equity Branch of the Department of the Prime Minister and Cabinet (DPMC).[4]

An important event in the Council's political environment was the 1997 release of the Human Rights and Equal Opportunity Commission's *Bringing Them Home* report on the "stolen generations" co-authored by former Justice of the High Court Sir Ronald Wilson.[5] Although a newspaper poll conducted immediately after the release showed that 70% of Australians favoured an apology to Indigenous Australians, Prime Minister John Howard quickly and firmly came out against an apology, on the grounds that it could open the government to massive compensation claims. Howard's refusal, of course, helped poison the atmosphere for reconciliation.

The Council conducted an extensive communications and outreach program. A major event was the Australian Reconciliation Convention, which was organized by the Council and held in Melbourne in May 1997, at the time of the tabling of the "stolen generations" report in Parliament. The Convention was attended by 1,800 participants. When the Prime Minister rose to speak, many delegates—both Indigenous and non-Indigenous—literally turned their back on him, much to his displeasure. While he did offer his personal sorrow on the stolen generations issue, he remained resolute in his refusal to issue a government apology. Instead, on May 26, 1998, the first National Sorry Day was held. Supported by the Council, it saw nearly a million people sign "sorry books."

In the years leading up to our focal period, Indigenous issues began to take on a much higher than normal profile. On December 23, 1996, the High Court issued its decision in the important *Wik* case on Native title.[6] That was followed by the

---

4. The Department of the Prime Minister and Cabinet (DPMC) is a separate entity from the Prime Minister's Office (PMO), just as in the Canadian federal government the Privy Council Office (PCO) and the Prime Minister's Office (PMO) are separate.

5. The "stolen generations" are primarily Australians of mixed Indigenous/non-Indigenous ancestry. They were taken from their Indigenous mothers, often while still infants, and placed in non-Indigenous adoptive homes. For an academic account of genocidal practices in Australia, see Kidd (1996).

6. The government's response to the *Wik* decision was called the "Ten Point Plan." Bachelard (1997) describes it as "the great land grab."

November 1997 announcement of the resignation of Indigenous leader Patrick Dodson as Chair of the Council (Kingston, 1997a) and by the Prime Minister's threat to call an election over the *Native Title Amendment Act* (Kingston, 1997b). Known colloquially as "the father of reconciliation," Dodson resigned in protest against the *Native Title Amendment Act* and the government's stance on reconciliation, including its response to the stolen generations report.[7] In his election night victory speech in October 1998, the Prime Minister again boosted the profile of Indigenous issues with a reaffirmation of his "commitment" to reconciliation. Said one interviewee (#1610) about the profile of Indigenous issues within the government and the Department of the Prime Minister and Cabinet, "I believe that neither the government nor higher levels of the Department took a special interest until [that speech]."

The Inner Circle and Other Actors

Although the Council made the decision to go ahead with the research, others were more intimately involved in the project. The term "inner circle" is used here to describe those who were most influential in the *design and strategic decision making* on the polling.

The project director was Brian Aarons, who headed the Communications Section of the Reconciliation and Equity Branch in the Department of the Prime Minister and Cabinet's Office of Indigenous Policy. In that position, he was the Council's Communications Director. He was the key liaison between the Council's secretariat in DPMC and the Council's executives, between the Council and the pollster, between the DPMC and the pollster, and between the Council and the media. He grew up in a politically left-wing family and, in his youth, was a political activist in the anti-war (Viet Nam) campaign. His longstanding involvement in Indigenous issues began with participation in the highly publicized 1965 Freedom Ride for Aboriginal rights. He holds an Honours bachelor's degree in sociology and another in physics and mathematics. Earlier in his career, he had edited a left-wing newspaper and had worked briefly for the Aboriginal and Torres Strait Islanders Commission (ATSIC) before making the move to work for the Council secretariat in 1994. In the secretariat, he had experience in the mid-1990s with one other survey and three focus group projects.

Also intimately involved was pollster John Davis of Newspoll Market Research. With a bachelor's degree in economic statistics and operations research, he brought to the project 22 years of experience in survey research, including some with rival Roy Morgan Research. It is worth noting that his employer, Newspoll, is partly owned by newspaper magnate Rupert Murdoch, who owns *The Australian*, among other papers. Newspoll does a great deal of voting intention and other

---

7. Aboriginal Affairs Minister John Herron described the removal of Indigenous children from their homes as "essentially lawful" and argued that there never was a *generation* of stolen children. See Kidd (2000).

public affairs survey work for the newspaper chain, and sometimes includes one or two questions on Indigenous issues. Newspoll also includes Indigenous issues as part of its regular polling calendar, in the form of a closed-ended question about the most important issues facing Australia. Thus, Davis had noteworthy, although not extensive, experience in the area.

Veteran opinion researcher Irving Saulwick also played an important role. He is one of the pioneers of public opinion research in Australia (Mills, 1986, p. 117). Although trained as an economist, he became critical of the paucity of sociological imagination in polling in Australia. So, early in his career, he convinced the Fairfax newspaper chain to support more sophisticated polling that could be reported in its two key newspapers, *The Age* (Melbourne) and the *Sydney Morning Herald*. From those quantitative beginnings, he branched into focus group work and consulting, including for government departments. With colleague Denis Muller, Saulwick was responsible for all of the focus group interviews done for the Council. Of course, he was heavily involved in constructing the discussion guides for those groups. During our focal period, Saulwick's participation in an early meeting with Aarons and Davis on the polling was important because the survey was intended, in part, to quantify the results and test the hypotheses from Saulwick's and Muller's focus groups in December 1999 and January 2000.

The other key member of the "inner circle" was Peter Vaughan. He was First Assistant Secretary in the DPMC's Office of Indigenous Policy. Vaughan, whose BA was in economics and English literature, was a veteran of twelve years in Indigenous program delivery in New South Wales. After a stint as a ministerial staffer and elsewhere in DPMC, in 1996 he took the First Assistant Secretary position. Although, formally, he reported to Jane Halton (described below), his work often brought him into direct dealings with ministers and the Prime Minister.

Meredith Fairweather was the Director of the Research and Communications Strategy Section in the Government Communications Unit at DPMC. Although her participation was not time intensive, it was sufficiently significant and diverse to include her in the inner circle. She had spent five years at the Australian Bureau of Statistics in its Populations Survey Design area, then eight years with a private sector research company (AGB McNair, now AC Nielsen) with particular involvement in survey and other operations. An experienced market researcher active in the quality standards work of the market researchers' professional association in Australia, she made important contributions to the polling questionnaire, the focus group discussion guide, and the selection of the research consultants.

Certain other individuals in DPMC were involved in the polling project, but their involvement was, for the most part, marginal. In terms of the concentric circles model used to describe involvement in the Nisga'a project, they would be considered to be in the second or, for some, even the third circle. They included Julie Yeend and Jane Halton. Yeend was Assistant Secretary in the Reconciliation and Equity Branch of the Office of Indigenous Policy. Brian Aarons reported to her and she reported to Peter Vaughan. Halton, as Executive Co-ordinator (Social Policy) in DPMC, reported to the Australian equivalent of Canada's Clerk of the Privy Council.[8] While not a major player in the public opinion research, she did attend virtually every meeting of Council during our focal period. Catherine Murphy, from the Prime Minister's Office (PMO), was described by one interviewee (#16062) as "John Howard's right hand person." As such, she might have been expected to be involved, but while she did attend certain Council meetings, she had negligible involvement in both the polling and focus group projects.

Outside of the DPMC and PMO, other members of the second and third ring of influence on the polling included opinion researcher Denis Muller and John Davis's colleagues at Newspoll, especially Lisa Fleming.

Although the Council's Chair and Deputy Chair were kept informed about the progress of the research, they did not play a strategic management role in the research. Significantly, Phillip Ruddock, the "inner cabinet" minister responsible for assisting the Prime Minister with reconciliation,[9] also was not involved in the polling and focus group work, despite exhibiting a keen interest in polling. Similarly, in British Columbia the Minister of Aboriginal Affairs was not involved in the polling and focus groups. However, Ruddock did attend portions of various Council meetings. The Prime Minister himself attended a number of special sessions of the Council, including the meeting of March 11, 2000 when a controversy surrounding leaked public opinion research findings was still very current.[10]

Polling and Focus Groups Around the "Document Toward Reconciliation"

The situations involving the sounding of public opinion on the Nisga'a Treaty and on the Australian *Document Toward Reconciliation* are similar in that both sponsors of the research were eager to discover responsive chords and the obstacles to acceptance of their respective project in the minds of members of the mass public. Substantial resources were devoted to public opinion research in both jurisdictions. In Australia, the public opinion research was also intended to hold up a mirror to the nation, and it came to be viewed within the Council as a fundamental and crucial part of the reconciliation process itself. How, they reasoned, could one talk about genuine reconciliation without understanding the public's actual views on a range of important issues related to reconciliation? The Council, therefore, devoted over $100,000 AUD in research contracts for late 1999 and early 2000.

---

8. Three division heads reported to Jane Halton, namely, Peter Vaughan (Office of Indigenous Policy) and the heads of the Office of the Status of Women and the Social Policy Division (responsible for health, education, welfare, etc.).

9. Later, Ruddock was appointed as Indigenous Affairs minister, per se.

10. The leaders of the three main federal political parties had been invited. Howard attended mainly to dialogue with Council members on general reconciliation issues and on the Council's *Draft Document for Reconciliation*. The issue of the leaks was not discussed at that meeting. Howard did not stay for the briefing on the survey results, perhaps because his "right hand person," Catherine Murphy, and Minister Ruddock had attended the Council's executive committee meeting in Sydney about a week earlier when the survey results had just been received.

Since its inception, CAR had conducted research of various kinds. For instance, its earlier public opinion research included tracking polls done using the Newspoll omnibus (multi-client) survey; focus group research conducted in January, February, and May 1996; and a quantitative survey done in June of that year. However, as noted, our focus is on the period from late 1999 through early 2000, in which the Council commissioned the following research:

- *Phase 1*: fourteen focus groups conducted throughout Australia between December 7, 1999 and January 13, 2000 by Irving Saulwick and Associates. This phase also included 23 in-depth interviews conducted during the same period with "leading citizens in 'high contact' areas."[11]
- *Phase 2*: a national telephone survey of 1,300 Australian adults, conducted from January 28 to February 14, 2000 by Newspoll Market Research.[12]
- *Phase 3*: a mail-out survey in which a copy of the *Draft Document Toward Reconciliation* was mailed to a subset of about half of the Phase 2 respondents. They were asked to complete a written questionnaire and then were telephoned to collect their answers. From the 650 asked to participate in this stage of the research, 280 usable replies were received.
- Phase 4: nine focus groups, involving only Indigenous persons, conducted throughout Australia during March and April 2000. This phase also included an unspecified number (at least six) of in-depth interviews with Indigenous elders, other Indigenous leaders, and other Indigenous persons. All interviews in this phase were conducted by Saulwick and Muller who describe themselves as "a couple of 'whitefellas'" (Saulwick and Muller, 2000b).

Outside our period of focal interest, in mid-February 2001, there was also a deliberative[13] poll held at the Old Parliament House in Canberra. The Council supported, in principle, the notion of such a deliberative poll, but the mid-February 2001 poll came after the Council ceased to exist. Hence, the Council did

---

11. For the discussion guide, interview guide, detailed results, and a description of the research, see Saulwick and Muller (2000a).

12. See Newspoll Market Research (2000) for a discussion of Phase 2 and Phase 3.

13. Deliberative polling seeks to examine what public opinion would be on a public policy issue when members of the public are placed together for a weekend and given an opportunity to be informed on the issue and to deliberate it with their peers. It involves randomly selected participants chosen, in the reconciliation deliberative poll, from across Australia. A baseline poll is conducted at the outset, in this case by Newspoll during the third week of November 2000. All 1,220 interviewees were invited to attend the all-expenses-paid weekend in Canberra. Carefully balanced briefing material is provided to participants. Under the guidance of trained moderators, participants deliberate on the issues in small groups and then are polled again at the end, in order to measure attitude change. For the reconciliation deliberative polling, the follow-up survey (N=334) was conducted by IDA in partnership with Newspoll. Proceedings of the deliberations are often broadcast, and the Australian Broadcasting Corporation (radio and TV) did carry parts of the reconciliation deliberation live or by tape.

not contribute to funding it. The poll was organized by a not-for-profit, non-partisan research organization called Issues Deliberation Australia (IDA).[14] It was preceded by eight "micro deliberations" held between early November 2000 and early February 2001 in regions where there are large numbers of Indigenous Australians. According to IDA, the regional deliberations aimed to facilitate the "informed voice" of Indigenous Australians, while the national deliberation aimed to facilitate the "informed voice" of all Australians. No counterpart to this deliberative polling was done on the Nisga'a Treaty.

Our attempt to understand the process of formulating, conducting, and reporting on public opinion research becomes more grounded if we have an appreciation for the flavour of the results of the soundings of public opinion in phases 1 through 4. We turn briefly to that now.

Overview of Results[15]

> Australians pride themselves on "mateship" and "a fair go for all mates." (Interviewee #16062)

Public opinion on Indigenous issues in Australia posed major challenges to the reconciliation initiative, the Council learned. Not only was a clear majority (57% to 62%, depending on the question) of the Australian population opposed to a government apology to Indigenous people, there was not even a consensus on the notion that Indigenous people are, generally speaking, "disadvantaged." Indeed, on the specific matter of "living conditions," only a slight majority of Australians perceived Indigenous people to be "worse off" or "a lot worse off" than other Australians, despite the fact that, as the Newspoll report says, Aboriginal and Torres Strait Islander people are "the poorest, unhealthiest, least-employed, worst-housed, and most-imprisoned Australians." Blaming the victim was widespread, for when asked to choose which of two statements "comes closest [sic] to how you feel" more people (47% v. 38%) chose "Aboriginal people have mainly themselves to blame for their current disadvantage" than chose "Disadvantage experienced by Aboriginal people today is mainly a result of the way they were treated in the past."

Opposition to "special" treatment of Indigenous Australians was strong and tinged with concerns about the financial costs of such treatment and the legal implications of an apology. Although a substantial majority agreed that there is a need for government programs to help reduce disadvantage among Aboriginal people, about the same proportion believed that Aboriginal people do not do enough to help themselves. Furthermore, there was a widespread perception that little had been achieved with previous efforts to assist Aboriginal people.

14. See <http://www.ida.org.au/hp.htm> (visited August 2, 2005), from which most of the information on the "Australia Deliberates: Reconciliation—Where From Here?" project was taken. I am also grateful to Dr. Pamela Ryan of IDA for information she provided on that project.

15. This section is based on Saulwick and Muller (2000a, 2000b) and Newspoll (2000).

The focus groups found that many non-Indigenous participants "missed the point" of the reconciliation initiative and the *Draft Document for Reconciliation.* They viewed the *Draft Document* to be divisive, backward looking, based only on an Aboriginal perspective, requiring a series of concessions from non-Aboriginal Australians without any corresponding "give" on the part of Aboriginal people, and a high risk document which would probably be used as the basis for claims for land and monetary compensation. Many exhibited an inability to imagine that other people might have fundamentally different ways of looking at life than they do. Many confused the issue of reconciliation with other Indigenous issues, such as welfare dependency, land rights, and assimilation. Behind many focus group members' statements, there was an intolerance or lack of empathy. Indeed, the very authenticity of Indigenous Australians who do not conform to stereotypes of Aboriginal people was challenged. Fortunately for the Council, the attitudes of the community leaders interviewed tended to be considerably more positive than those found in the focus groups.

The empirical findings of the survey were not all negative for the Council's mandate. Although acceptance of the *Draft Document for Reconciliation* in its entirety was the exception rather than the rule, about three quarters of those who read it reported supporting most or all of the *Document.* Another positive finding for the Council was that a large majority regarded reconciliation as important, and a majority agreed that the nation should formally acknowledge "Aboriginal people as the original owners of traditional lands and waters" and "that Australia was occupied without the consent of Aboriginal people."

The focus groups with Indigenous Australians yielded some findings on points of potential convergence in the views of Indigenous and non-Indigenous Australians and some findings on the gulf still separating them. One of the points of convergence was that the past should be confronted and acknowledged and a fuller history of Australia be taught in the schools. Another was that there should be both an acknowledgement of past wrongs and an expression of genuine regret, without today's Australians taking personal blame. Among the points of profound disagreement across the "racial" divide were views on "special treatment," views on the emotionally sensitive issue of the "stolen generations," and certain points in the draft document, such as recognition of customary Indigenous law and traditions. These examples attest to the magnitude of the challenge faced by the Council even at that late date in its mandate.

Tension Within the DPMC and With the Council

> Council members were quite incensed by the leak of the Saulwick report. (Interviewee #16062)

Prime Minister Howard made a point of stressing the independence of the Council, and relations between the Council's secretariat and the upper echelons of DPMC were generally constructive, although characterized by palpable tension in some quarters. Decision making within the secretariat was driven by what the Council decided rather than by the DPMC's responsibilities to the government of the day and its policies. As Brian Aarons said,

> In my role as the Council's Communications Director, my responsibilities were clear and accepted by all so far as I knew. As all of us on the Council staff sat here in the Prime Minister's Department, our role was to carry out the Council's policy and to advise it as to how best to implement that policy. In my case, I would, for example, draft media releases according to Council's policy and not any other consideration.
>
> This was the case even where there was a gap, often a big gap, between the Council's policy and the policy of the government of the day ... If the Council Chairperson told me to write a speech or media release criticizing the government, it was my job to do so. It was also expected that I would notify the Prime Minister's Office— and this was understood by the Council and its Chair.

Thus, the secretariat's mandate was a somewhat bifurcated one: it served primarily the independent Council; yet, as public servants, secretariat members also served the government. Notwithstanding Aarons's remarks, there were some very important occasions when strains in the relations did adversely impinge on the processing (including gathering and disseminating) of public opinion on reconciliation. They are the focus of this section, along with relations between DPMC and the Council.

In the British Columbia situation, the conflict between John Heaney and Shawn Thomas was over the means to achieve a shared, high priority goal. In contrast, in the Australian situation, the Prime Minister and the Council shared neither the same vision of reconciliation nor the same sense of priority. Therefore, the potential for the Council's work and research to create political embarrassment and other political difficulty for the Prime Minister was high. The delegates turning their backs on the Prime Minister at the Reconciliation Convention demonstrated that fact. Furthermore, a latent tension was inherent in the very structural arrangements, which saw the Council's secretariat housed within the Department of the Prime Minister and Cabinet (DPMC). Although formally it was clear that the secretariat had a dual mandate to work for the Council and to advise the government, the issue of to whom secretariat staff members owed their primary loyalty—the Council or DPMC—was bound to arise, and it did eventually, as in British Columbia. Indeed, the somewhat awkward position that secretariat members occupied in the Australian government structure had parallels to the position in which non-partisan public servants on the Nisga'a project found themselves in British Columbia. Recall the quotation from Shawn Thomas about resisting partisan political pressure from the NDP government.

BOX 8.1
Evidence of Close Involvement of the DPMC in the Public Opinion Research: Peter Vaughan's Written Input

The following are examples of comments written by First Assistant Secretary of the Office of Indigenous Policy, Peter Vaughan, on various documents containing draft questions and procedures for the public opinion research surrounding the *Document Toward Reconciliation.*

- "I'd like to see the final instrument before we agree to it." (Nov. 16/99, re: telephone polling questionnaire)
- "I have strong doubts about the value of the mailout questionnaire." (Jan. 17/00)
- "Not relevant. Delete" (Jan. 17/00, re: Q5)
- "2 different concepts mixed up here" (Jan. 17/00, re: Q7b)
- "A very vague concept" (Jan. 17/00, re: Q7h)
- "Too technical and bureaucratic to elicit a meaningful response. Delete" (Jan. 17/00, re: Q8a–d)
- "50% of 1600 = 800. Even a 50% (unlikely?) response rate among that 800 will result in a sample far too small to be statistically valid or meaningful." (Jan. 17/00, re: attempt to get 50% of telephone respondents to participate in Phase 3)
- "What's the point of this question?" (Jan. 21/00, re: question on importance of Aboriginal issues)
- "Crude but effective(!)" (Jan. 21/00, re: question asking respondents' degree of agreement or disagreement with the statement "Compared with other Australians, Aborigines get too many handouts from government." Phraseology later revised.)
- "A pointless question: the answer to 10 or 11 ... tells you this." (Jan. 21/00, re: question 12 on the preferred name for the Reconciliation document)
- "...The Q on 'special rights' MUST go in" (Jan. 25/00, re: telephone survey)
- "I think this will be a waste of time and resources. The likely respondent will be the strong supporters and strong opponents. Won't capture the middle" (Feb./00, re: mail-out survey)

Source: Various documents obtained in response to Freedom of Information request by Senator John Faulkner.

In light of the above, it is not surprising that DPMC documents demonstrate that the public opinion research commanded careful attention among DPMC executives. Indeed, the documents cited below show that one of those executives, Peter Vaughan, was intimately involved in vetting potential questions. Like Doug McArthur in British Columbia, Vaughan provided detailed input on questions across various drafts of the questionnaire. Vaughan also made certain methodological demands pertaining to sampling. With some experience in government polling on controversial issues and many years experience in DPMC, Vaughan was not bashful in his comments. Remarks that he wrote on the documents are illustrated in Box 8.1.

As Box 8.1 shows, Vaughan was insistent that a particularly controversial question on "special rights" be included in the telephone survey. The final version of the question at issue read as follows: "It's been suggested that as the original

Australians, Aboriginal people should be entitled to special rights like native title, or special seats in Parliament. Do you personally think that Aboriginal people should, or should not have special rights such as these?"[16] Vaughan's "advice" was followed, despite objections from several quarters, including Newspoll's John Davis. The controversy surrounding the question was multifaceted. For instance, in addition to the allegation of "rigging" the question to elicit replies unsympathetic to Indigenous people, there was the technical problem of the pollster's felt need for a long preamble to the question, for the issue of "special" Indigenous rights is much broader than just Native title and designated seats in Parliament. In addition, there was the issue of factual inaccuracy, for DPMC was advised that Native title in Australia is a common law right, rather than a "special" right. A January 25, 2000 memo to file written by Julie Yeend reveals divisions over the question within the executive ranks of DPMC and with the pollster, John Davis. Yeend wrote,

> I discussed the question with Ms Halton late this afternoon & she said that the native title reference should be removed if it was inaccurate. In further conversations with John Davis tonight, I put this view, but we both agreed that special seats in Parl. is far too narrow a concept for the broad issue being tested. Also, that formulation is more likely to have a negative skew as there are many who support the concept of native title. Recognizing its flaw, I told John D. to go ahead with both the native title and special seats elements in the question.

As in British Columbia and elsewhere in Canada, the use of the phrase "special rights" in Australian polling depresses support for the statement in which it is found, for "special rights" are perceived as violating widely shared and strongly held values of equality (in Australia, "mateship" or "a fair go for all mates"). Thus, Vaughan's insistence on the inclusion of the "special rights" question was construed by the Opposition in Parliament as bordering on what the Australians call "push-polling"—which is to say, asking "slanted" or "loaded" questions to obtain a desired result (in Canadian parlance, "cooking the poll"). In speaking to a motion to censure the Minister of Aboriginal Affairs (Senator Herron), Senator Faulkner focused on the telephone survey and this "special rights" question in particular. He accused the Minister of being "involved in a long term strategy of driving a wedge of racism through the community" and of "corrupting the Reconciliation polling process." Referring to Vaughan by his position title, Faulkner added,

---

16. Earlier drafts of the question also included reference to Indigenous "customary law." On the final version of the question, 58% of respondents opposed "special rights" while 36% favoured such rights, and 7% were coded as "neither/don't know."

[He] and the Prime Minister's own office knew full well that the public is susceptible to questions on special rights—whether treaties, or compensation, or in this case his demand for a gratuitous question on special seats for Aborigines in Parliament—an issue that has really not featured in the whole of the reconciliation debate. It's the old Mark Textor trick, a technique imported from the Northern Territory and the CLP—it is divisive and frankly it borders on push polling.[17]

Vaughan was not only insistent about the inclusion of the "special rights" question but also very sceptical about the representativeness of persons who came forth to speak at the public consultation meetings organized by the Council. In addition, he was vigilant on sampling issues, in contrast to our political players in British Columbia where sampling was treated as a merely technical matter and a non-issue. For instance, Vaughan consulted survey research expert Dr. Roger Jones, formerly of the Social Science Data Archive at the Australian National University, on one sampling issue (margin of error) of particular concern to him. Then, on a document pertaining to the focus group research among Indigenous people and dated February 21, 2000, Vaughan wrote the following: "OK but it all hinges on the reliability of the group recruited. Need to be very circumspect. Make sure we know (after, if not before) who the recruiters are and do some checking on them." Here we can discern perhaps something less than full trust in the Council's research agenda. This researcher is left with the impression that Vaughan regarded the Council as somewhat of a "loose cannon," which is to say by no means fully in the government's fold and therefore potentially damaging.

Having used up some political capital with his stance on the "special rights" question, Vaughan did not exercise his veto power over the use of the mail-out survey, even though he was of the strong opinion that the mail-out survey would be worthless.

Another issue contributing to tension between DPMC, on the one hand, and the Council and its secretariat, on the other hand, was leaks. Strategic leaks in the Indigenous affairs realm were not a rarity during the life of the Council. Among the most noteworthy leaks were these:

- the focus group results on the commercials prepared (not for the Council) in support of the government's Ten Point Plan on Native title;
- selected results of the March 1998 tri-state (Queensland, Western Australia, Northern Territory) governments' survey on Native title issues;

17. Senator Faulkner's remarks are from a document entitled "Herron Censure—Right of Reply" dated April 10, 2000. The document, included in the government's response to Senator Faulkner's Freedom of Information request, is an excerpt of a transcript of a parliamentary session, although it is not clear if it is a session of the Senate or of a parliamentary committee. Mark Textor is the pollster to the Prime Minister. CLP refers to the right-wing Country Labor Party in the Northern Territory.

- the Council's February 1999 *Draft Document for Reconciliation*;
- the focus group results contained in the February 2000 report ("the Saulwick report") by Irving Saulwick & Associates and Denis Muller & Associates;[18] and
- the final report of the Council.

The fourth of these leaks was very damaging to reconciliation and CAR. For instance, media coverage dwelled on the strong and "widespread" opposition to a government apology to Indigenous people. Indeed, some thought that the leak of the Saulwick report would be the death knell for the Council. The leak incensed Council members and certainly forced the Council into "damage control" mode whereby it sought to manage reactively the interpretations of the Saulwick findings. The leak of the focus group results before the survey results were ready pre-empted the Council from proactively managing the combined findings of the opinion research projects with its own interpretive "spin." As one interviewee (#16062) said about the leak, "We had all the negative information out, but nothing from the community consultations to balance it, nor the Newspoll [survey] results."

Coincidence or not, the leak of the Saulwick results occurred at the same time as the Prime Minister's public reneging on his commitment to attain reconciliation by the centenary of the founding of the federation (Shanahan, 2000). Coming only about twelve months after the leak of the Council's draft reconciliation document, the leak of the focus group results fuelled distrust in the trilateral relationship between the secretariat, the Council, and the rest of DPMC, for DPMC staff and even secretariat staff were obvious targets of suspicion as the possible leaker(s).

A further issue that significantly strained relations between higher echelons of DPMC and the Council's secretariat was the release of Minister John Herron's response, on behalf of the government, to the "stolen generations" report. That response came in April 2000, without any advance briefing to the Council or the secretariat, such that their members were left at the mercy of mass media reporters seeking their reactions. The government's denial of the "stolen generation" was like a slap in the face to the reconciliation effort. Readily interpretable as "blaming the victim," it had a strong polarizing effect. This was "wedge politics" (Kingston, 2000b) writ large, but unlike the British Columbia government's use of wedge politics on the Nisga'a Treaty issue, the agenda of the Howard government was profoundly anti-Indigenous. Commentary in the newspapers bespeaks the furore and crisis-like atmosphere created by the government's stance. Indigenous senator Aden Ridgeway accused the government of "throwing an incendiary into race relations" and "watching it go off, to see how much harm you can do" and added that "only the most racist person would be unsympathetic to the plight of the stolen generations" (Seccombe, 2000). Indigenous leader Charles Perkins was

---

18. See, for instance, Dennis Shanahan's February 28, 2000 article in *The Australian*; the March 3, 2000 newspaper article by Michelle Grattan and Margo Kingston in the *Sydney Morning Herald (SMH)*; and Margo Kingston's solo piece on March 3, 2000 in *SMH*.

quoted as saying "It's burn, baby burn, from now on. Anything can happen," and Peter Yu, Executive Director of the Kimberly Land Council asserted that the Howard government wanted to return to "a terra nullius of the spirit" (Stephens, 2000). Former High Court justice Sir Ronald Wilson, the author of the original "stolen generations" report in 1997, publicly stated that he was appalled by the government's denial that there had been a generation of stolen Indigenous children. He added, "Not only was the [Herron] submission factually flawed, but the sheer insult it conveyed was devastating. It was totally hurtful" (Farrant, 2000). He went on to say that the Prime Minister's "extraordinary 1950s attitudes" meant that there could be no serious advances in reconciliation while he was in office (Farrant, 2000). From these reactions, it is obvious that the Herron response put the Council in a very awkward position. Not surprisingly, it left Council members decidedly angry.

To summarize, at strategically important points, collegial accountability in the DPMC was set aside. In particular,

- Peter Vaughan "pulled rank" to insist on certain approaches or content,
- sampling representativeness was impugned, and
- leaks or vital announcements were deployed in a manner that gave the appearance of an offensive strike to undermine the Council's goals and work.

Trust and the ability of the Council to achieve its goals suffered. This situation stands in marked contrast to the British Columbia situation. There, the inner circle experienced conflict over strategy, but there were no leaks. The public opinion data did not become a weapon in internal organizational politics within the BC government. Furthermore, the sense of "religious" zeal for the Treaty among members of the BC inner circle, a zeal that was not widely shared in Australia's DPMC (beyond the Council secretariat), provided a degree of unity that transcended distrust among insiders in the BC project.

Agonizing Over Every Word: Questionnaire Origin and Construction

The Australian polling research was born, in part, out of a desire to "hold a mirror up to the nation." It was the Council's responsibility to ascertain where Australians stood on the issues, including their prejudices, areas of ignorance, and emphases. These would have to be taken into consideration when making recommendations on the strategy for reconciliation and when composing the final draft of the *Document Toward Reconciliation.*

Politically, it is very significant that the polling research was also born out of a concern about possible bias in the feedback received in the Council's extensive public consultation meetings.[19] By Council estimates, a combined total of over ten

---

19. Interview with P. Vaughan and CAR Agenda Paper No. 2, entitled "Proposal to Upgrade Social Research," created for its Executive Committee Meeting of September 17, 1999.

thousand Indigenous and non-Indigenous Australians participated in those July through November 1999 consultations. Nevertheless, data from a representative national sample were deemed necessary in order to demonstrate that Council had obtained the views of the wider community. Both the Council's executive committee and the Council itself supported the proposal for the research, and it went through with little discussion (#1610).

Newspoll was chosen as the data collection firm in a commonly used limited tender process that, in this case, saw six firms invited to bid. Of the five bids received, Newspoll's was deemed by the selection committee (Aarons, Yeend, and Fairweather) to have met best the specified selection criteria. The fact that Newspoll was seen as the pre-eminent polling firm in Australia in its sampling techniques and in the accuracy of its election predictions was a bonus. One does not want one's findings called into question on methodological grounds, especially in light of the fact that research done for the Council in the mid-1990s had already suffered under such methodological critique.

In both British Columbia and Australia, construction of the polling questionnaires was a highly collaborative process in which the pollster played a pivotal role. Operating under tight time constraints and with various individuals absent due to Christmas and summer vacations,[20] Newspoll short-circuited some of its usual standard operating procedures. The Freedom of Information documents reveal that a flurry of faxes crossed the wires between the Newspoll offices in Sydney and Brian Aarons in the Council's secretariat in Canberra. Newspoll's John Davis, working with colleague Lisa Fleming, took a very "hands-on" approach to this highly sensitive questionnaire instrument. Said Davis, "An awful lot of time went into it. I've never spent so much time agonizing over every word and every question.... I can't impress on you enough the amount of time and thought that went into it." Part of the commitment of time also involved Newspoll's attendance at two focus groups hosted by Saulwick and Muller, respectively, in Sydney.[21]

In a manner akin to what was found in the Nisga'a case study, the questionnaire evolved iteratively from a rough overview of topic areas proposed by Newspoll. It was subjected to intense scrutiny, debate, and proposed revisions before reaching its final contested form. Along the way, Peter Vaughan identified a list of his priority topics for inclusion, most of which had already been proposed. Documents released in response to Senator Faulkner's Freedom of Information request reveal that Aarons kept Vaughan and Julie Yeend abreast of the evolving questionnaire, and there were several opportunities for their input. Yeend was extraordinarily busy with other work at the time, such that her input was negligible,

---

20. "After the middle of December, you can forget about Australia, until mid-January at least," said one interviewee.

21. Julie Yeend and Jackie Huggins, an Indigenous member of the Council, attended a focus group session in Brisbane. The procedure is for such observers to watch from behind a two-way mirror, but for the participants to be told that they are there.

except on the "special rights" question.[22] The final draft of the questionnaire was provided to the Chair and Deputy Chair of the Council. However, they were not briefed on the disagreement over the "special rights" question and the fact that it could be construed as an intervention by DPMC in favour of the government and its policy. The Council members, all but one of whom were part time, gave generously of their time but seldom had the time to get involved in the fine details of the secretariat's work. Thus, in light of the tight time constraints, they were given the questionnaire (and the discussion guide for the focus groups) mainly for information purposes rather than for deliberation or approval.

As noted earlier, Irving Saulwick was co-author of the focus group report whose results the polling exercise was, in part, intended to quantify. Saulwick was an important contributor to the construction of the polling questionnaire. He was able to provide insights from those focus groups and also argued the case for some different formatting of some important questions (e.g., forced choice versus Likert scale), including at least one that met with the objections of some members of Council when they finally saw it at the results reporting stage.

Political and bureaucratic insiders engaged in public opinion research are sometimes wary of even the possibility of Freedom of Information requests from political opponents, journalists, or others, for such requests have the potential to create political or legal difficulties. That potential is inherent in subject matter as sensitive as relations between Indigenous people and the larger society. According to my Australian interviewees, Freedom of Information requests were not at all a consideration in questionnaire construction. In part, this was because the results were to be released publicly and were to be held up to the nation as a "mirror" in which the nation could see itself. However, Peter Vaughan was "burned" badly when Senator Faulkner's Freedom of Information request yielded documents (discussed above) containing Vaughan's written remarks that were politically embarrassing to the government. One might assume that Freedom of Information considerations will loom larger in the DPMC's work on draft questionnaires in the future.

Sampling: Social Control, Presentation of Self, and the "Fred X" Factor

Scattered references to sampling considerations have already been made. The reader will recall that sampling considerations emerged as both an issue and, to a limited but significant extent, an instrument of social control. Clearly, among political actors, sampling integrity or adequacy also became an important part of what sociologists call "the presentation of self." This is illustrated in the Phase 1 focus groups, where considerations of political "optics" led to the selection of a sample that was geographically more dispersed around Australia than was

---

22. Yeend was involved, though, in the Saulwick focus group research. She provided an in-depth briefing to Saulwick on the purpose of the research and observed at least one focus group session in person.

otherwise deemed necessary. In that sense, sampling was strategic, and it is important that we understand sampling as a tool ("weapon" might be too strong a word) in situations of actual or potential conflict. That is to say, a sample drawn in conformity with methodological canons or "bulked up" in particular geographic areas can be effective both in disarming potential critics and in making the case that the results from one's own research are more valid than those from another's research.

Sampling representativeness as an issue also emerged with regard to the Phase 4 focus groups. The point is well illustrated in the remarks of Peter Vaughan, who discussed the recruiters of Indigenous participants in those focus groups:

> That was a minor reservation there. We've had [projects] where the recruiters will see someone's name, like Fred X, in a newspaper and assume that he's more representative or has more influence or status in the community than he or she actually does and then go off and use Fred X as their conduit into the community or their main point of reference or their main contact or whatever. We've seen that happen time and time again ... I had an apprehension or worry that when they went out to do the Aboriginal focus groups that they might unwittingly end up in the hands of Fred X ... and Fred X's sub-group. With our very small number of encounter groups, two or three instances of that kind could really sorta skew the whole exercise.

Public opinion research is, in significant part, about reducing political uncertainty and enhancing the public presentation of political actors and their projects. The Australian case suggests that those actors should be attentive to the possibility that the public opinion research could prove counter-productive if strategic considerations around sampling are neglected.

The Data Enter the Organization: Circulation and Briefing

The data came into DPMC and the Council via Brian Aarons. He provided the preliminary tables from the Newspoll report to Peter Vaughan and Julie Yeend and the draft Saulwick report to Vaughan, in both instances before the results went to the Council. The preliminary Newspoll results were kept under lock and key by Aarons.

The Prime Minister's Office was more than eager to see the quantitative results,[23] as were other political leaders who knew about the research. Eventually the secretariat relented and arranged advance release of those results to the leaders

---

23. That eagerness is evident in a document provided in response to Senator Faulkner's Freedom of Information request, namely, CAR's Agenda Paper No. 10, Meeting 36, March 10–12, 2000, entitled "Update Report on Social Research."

of the three main federal parties, and to selected journalists on the promise that they would abide by a brief embargo on any publication of the findings.

The Council received a detailed and very frank briefing on the Phase 1 focus group findings from Muller. (Saulwick was ill.) Many of the non-Indigenous Council members reportedly were shocked at the racism that Muller related. Yet, the two-hour PowerPoint briefing on the Newspoll quantitative survey results was a more emotional session. On the one hand, it involved much more animated discussion, as some Council members, speaking from a very pro-Aboriginal position, attacked John Davis over at least three questions (on special rights, disadvantage, and living conditions) that they considered to have been phrased in a manner biased against Indigenous people. They took issue with the meaning being attached to some questions and demanded to know who authored certain questions. Irving Saulwick was present at that same session, though, and had quite a different impact on the Council members. His persona itself, as an elderly gentleman, resonated with Indigenous members of Council, who welcomed him like a respected elder.[24] Then, his account of early results from the Phase 4 Indigenous focus groups brought tears to the eyes of some Council members. One person in attendance also described some Council members at this meeting as being very distraught at the state of race relations and the challenges of getting race relations on the government's agenda.

In his briefing of Council on the survey results, Newspoll's Davis was operating under the philosophy of just presenting the results and leaving the interpreting to others. However, his own interpretation of the results did lead him to proffer the advice that whatever Council does going forward must not be seen as "more of the same." Indeed, Council did later seek (unsuccessfully) to have the Prime Minister make some bold, "circuit breaker" move on reconciliation.

"These Are Not Simple Issues": Interpretation and Use of the Data

The leaked results of the Saulwick report were easily interpreted as very negative for reconciliation. Said one insider (#1610),

> I do think that, had the Council been allowed to manage the release itself, it could have been done with a more positive and objective spin on it.[25] But ... you can't get away from the fact half of Australians

24. The respect was mutual. In a development reminiscent of Peter Lanyon's experience among the Nisga'a, Saulwick himself was impressed by what he described as the "profound sense of spirituality" that he encountered among Indigenous people while conducting his research. He noted, "It would be absolutely wrong to not comment on that," and his report (Saulwick & Muller, 2000b, pp. 23–25) does go into considerable detail on his group's time with the Elders of Elcho Island, NT.

25. An example of such a positive spin is provided in comments made by Irving Saulwick at the media briefing, when he emphasized the "ifs" in saying that Australians have a concern about an apology *if* they are made to feel guilty about it and *if* there are implications for compensation.

don't believe Aboriginal people are disadvantaged and roughly 60%
don't think we should offer an apology. That's a fact, and then the
real issue is what you then do.

An interpretation that gained some currency within the Council was that the
results showed the supporters of reconciliation what the actual situation was and
that they needed to work more on it. Similarly, the interpretation placed on the
results by editorialists and political commentators was that the results called out
for opinion leadership from the Prime Minister. Interviewee #1610 went on to
say,

> Most of the commentators and editorials are saying "This goes
> to show that more should be done." Several commentators said,
> "What's needed here is leadership." It's interesting. If you take the
> Newspoll results overall, the sort of contradictoriness and fluidity
> of people's views indicate that. These are not simple issues we're
> dealing with.

When the government's response to the "stolen generations" report was leaked
to *The Daily Telegraph* a little over a month after the leak of the Saulwick findings,
the combined effect was to give credence to journalists' interpretations that the
government was in crisis on Indigenous issues generally.

In their draft report on the Phase 1 focus group findings, Saulwick and Muller
offered interpretations of their findings for the Council's communications strategy. Brian Aarons reined them in somewhat, for they were offering those interpretations in the absence of the polling data and in ignorance of some of Council's
earlier work. They had, in his view, exceeded the terms of reference governing
their contract.[26] Significantly, even though Aarons was the project director, he was
constrained by social norms that militate against interfering with the autonomy
of outside professional consultants. Hence, only some of the material in question
was removed. Said Aarons,

> I didn't say, "This should just go out altogether" or "It's got to be
> written how I say." I simply ameliorated some of the more ill-in-
> formed and more extreme ways they stated things. I did say to both
> of them that they need to be very careful it didn't look like they were
> trying to tell the Council what to do, particularly since we didn't
> have the quantitative results. And they took that point on board....
> Both lots of researchers [Saulwick/Muller and Newspoll], in their
> own way, and it's explicit in the Saulwick-Muller report; they more

---

26. Says political journalist Stephen Mills (1986, p. 81), "According to [pollster] Sweeney,
Australian qualitative researchers tend to be 'a little more creative, a little more ballsy' in writing their reports than Americans, going out on a limb to interpret meaning for the client."

or less say, "Well, the *Declaration* should be withdrawn and this should happen and that should happen, etc." They raised this issue, and I ameliorated that a bit. It was really quite strong initially. In my view, they had over-reacted and panicked on the basis of their own very personal experiences in the focus groups and didn't quite understand that Council had a number of options open to it, including the option of voluntary commitments by people to this document.... John Davis [of Newspoll] said to me, "Look, I don't know what you may want to make of this, but if this was a product like a normal product, on the basis of the research results I'd say to the client, 'Well, you'd withdraw the product.'" And I said, "Well, ... of course, it's not quite like that; it's not a product; it's a complex social and political *process*."

Saulwick's take on his exchanges with Aarons bespoke no sense of heavy-handedness from Aarons:

I went through some cases in which suggestions were made to me, some of which I accepted and some of which I didn't.... Brian was the only one who argued with me, and I don't think, in his case, it was political pressure. I think in his case it was genuine dialogue about the best way of expressing what I wanted to express. But I didn't feel any political pressure and that's different.... I was happy to pull back a bit there [re: recommendations]. I think there might have been a paragraph or two [removed], which I really didn't think was terribly important, but we really did put in most of the substance of what we wanted to say even though we'd gone a bit beyond our brief [mandate]. I don't think there was anything [by way of changes requested] really of substance. I think I left in one paragraph that Brian was worried about. He's a good man, Brian.

When explicitly asked later, Saulwick recounted that Aarons was not trying to negotiate over the actual meaning attached to the findings. He went on to corroborate Aarons: "There was never any statement such as 'I don't think you ought to say that' or 'It's not proper to say that' or 'That is better left unsaid.' Never any of that sort of 'Don't rock the boat by saying that.'"

Another important area of interpretation was the outcome on the "special rights" question. The 35% support for "special rights" as portrayed in the question was widely interpreted in the press as a bleak sign for reconciliation. However, within the secretariat, the fact that *as many as* 35% supported "special rights" *even on a question loaded against a pro-Aboriginal stance*, was seen as good news or at least as more positive than it might seem at first glance.

Some interpretation of findings involves making a value judgement as to their practical significance. That is seen in the following comments of Peter Vaughan:

The survey has caused us to re-think some things about Indigenous affairs. For instance, I didn't realize the extent to which attitudes had hardened [as we see, for example] in the response to that disadvantage question.... The most dramatic revelation in the survey, to my mind, was that the general public doesn't buy the notion that the situation of Aboriginal people today is a result of history rather than individual responsibility. That surprised me.

In both British Columbia and Australia, the survey and focus group data were not allowed to dictate policy. Thus, the British Columbia government was not going to allow public opinion to change the negotiated Treaty or to push the government into agreeing to hold a referendum on the Treaty. In Australia, the Council for Aboriginal Reconciliation was, in principle, not willing to allow public opinion to dictate the content of the *Document Toward Reconciliation*. One specific example of this principle in practice involved the use of the word "treaty." Council members who suggested that Council should take account of the polling results surrounding this word did not carry the day.[27] Instead, the Australian polling results were used mainly for "holding up a mirror to the nation" and for briefing Council members in preparation for public speaking engagements. Indeed, the project director's own assessment was that, although the public opinion research was valuable even as just an historical record, if the Council had not had the public opinion research results, it probably would not have done anything differently than it did.

In both BC and Australia, in order to assess public opinion on the issues, the politicians relied on a much broader variety of inputs than just polling and focus groups. Indeed, those other (non-systematic) sources were deemed by politicians to be highly reliable. Thus, in Australia, a common answer to my question about whether there likely would be an increase in polling on Indigenous issues in the future was that this would be unlikely to occur. The reason usually given was that the government feels it knows non-Indigenous opinion already.[28] The interpretation being implicitly applied here is that public opinion on Indigenous issues is fairly stable.

---

27. The final question on the survey questionnaire asked whether the reconciliation document "should only be a statement of principles and goals to guide future relations OR the principles and goals in the document should be made legally enforceable through a treaty or Act of Parliament." Although only 28% favoured the treaty rights approach while over 60% favoured non-enforceability, the final *Document Toward Reconciliation* did not shy away from a discourse of rights. For instance, it contains the clause "We recognize this land and its waters were settled as colonies without treaty or consent," the clause "We desire a future where all Australians enjoy their rights," and the clause "... we pledge ourselves to ... respect that Aboriginal and Torres Strait Islander peoples have the right to self-determination within the life of the nation."

28. Another reason given was that Indigenous issues are not "top of mind" issues in the public. They regularly receive a low score in survey questions asking about the most important issues facing Australia.

"People Need to be Persuaded": Postscript on What Happened on Reconciliation

Although the reconciliation process itself is not a focal concern of this chapter, it is perhaps appropriate to conclude this chapter with a thumbnail sketch of what has happened with reconciliation in Australia since the cessation of my research.[29] The deliberative polling of early 2001 has already been mentioned and will not be discussed here.

On May 27, 2000, the Council for Aboriginal Reconciliation sponsored Corroboree 2000. This grand gesture of reconciliation included "handing over" to the people of Australia the *Document Toward Reconciliation* at the famous Sydney Opera House. In addition, the next day, approximately one third of a million Australians, including a quarter million in Sydney alone, participated in bridge crossings to signify their support for reconciliation. Hundreds of thousands of others participated in other bridge walks over the next few months in other cities and towns. The cumulative total was about one million persons and, pointedly, did not include Prime Minister Howard (though a walk of about 300,000 people in Melbourne in late 2000 included Howard's Liberal Party Deputy Leader and federal Treasurer, Peter Costello).

Perhaps buoyed by the Saulwick and Newspoll findings, the Prime Minister held to his refusal to issue a formal government apology.[30] Indeed, he abandoned his election night promise of putting in place measures to implement reconciliation by the 2001 centenary of the federation that established Australia.[31] On May 11, 2000, he released his own version (Howard, 2000) of a reconciliation statement— a version that he said his government could have supported. Indeed, in some important respects, the government and the Council were not terribly far apart in their preferred phraseologies. As one observer who was close to the deliberations opined, "If it had not been for stubbornness by some non-Indigenous Council members on some minor matters of political correctness, it is quite possible that we could have had a document that Howard would have agreed to."

For his failure to play a more meaningful leadership role in reconciliation, the Prime Minister was roundly criticized. The *Sydney Morning Herald* editorial of March 6, 2000 captured the essence of the issue as follows: "People need to be persuaded, as Mr. Howard well knows, on most great policy issues."

As per the sunset clause in *The Council for Aboriginal Reconciliation Act, 1991,* the Council for Aboriginal Reconciliation was disbanded, effective January 1, 2001. The "Conclusions" chapter of its Final Report (Council for Aboriginal

---

29. Much of this section is taken from the *Reconciliation Australia Profile 2005* report available at <www.reconciliationaustralia.org> (accessed August 3, 2005).

30. Some close observers believe that the Prime Minister would have maintained his refusal to issue an apology regardless of poll results.

31. Speculation in some quarters was that Howard's abandoning of his election night reconciliation promise was intended to dampen the expectations of Council members before they painted him into a more difficult political corner.

Reconciliation, 2000) identified fifty-nine conclusions and principles about rec-onciliation, of which six (#s 10, 17, 18, 22, 35, and 40) dealt with public opinion in terms of attitudes, awareness, beliefs, and the need for education.

The Council put Indigenous issues, reconciliation, and the nation's responsi-bility to do something constructive about reconciliation "on the map" of Australians' consciousness. As Professor Margaret Reynolds, a Council member, said in the Final Report (Appendix 5), "After 10 years reconciliation has become an integral part of the Australian psyche." To build on that and continue the work of reconciliation, the Council created Reconciliation Australia. It is an independent, not-for-profit foundation co-chaired by a former member of the Council, Indig-enous academic Ms Jackie Huggins. The mission of the foundation is to promote and build reconciliation. To that end, it promotes awareness, facilitates partner-ships between Indigenous and non-Indigenous organizations (business, govern-mental, religious, and civil society), demystifies reconciliation, combats racism, attempts to shape public policy and *influence public opinion*, and works to improve the way public and private institutions engage with Indigenous communities. The foundation also supports and promotes good practice projects that can serve as models, and it researches the impact of different strategies for bringing about change. Examples of specific activities in which the foundation engages include co-sponsoring the annual Indigenous Governance Awards and the annual Rec-onciliation Day, involving youth in coming together across the racial divide, and continuing to work toward a national agreement for a shared future. Significantly, the work of the foundation has involved the establishment of working relation-ships with Neil Sterritt, a prominent Indigenous leader from British Columbia, and with the Harvard University Indigenous Governance project that captivated senior officials in Canada's Department of Indian Affairs and Northern Develop-ment around the same time.

Chapter Nine: Summary and Conclusion

At the outset, I noted that the research reported herein is guided by certain premises loosely derived from symbolic interactionist theory and social constructionist theory (Blumer, 1969; Holstein & Miller, 2003; Spector & Kitsuse, 1977). The first premise was that there is nothing automatic about the registering of public opinion with decision makers. Rather, we need to problematize each aspect of the process of gathering, interpreting, and registering public opinion. For instance, public opinion findings are not just a product (a report) handed to decision makers. Instead, the registering of public opinion with decision makers is a social process influenced by social and political factors such as trust, confidence, and norms of professionalism, among others. Furthermore, decision makers are not necessarily aloof bystanders; rather, they can be intimately involved in influencing the public opinion gathering and shaping efforts. Thus, I maintained, the processes involved in deciding to conduct a poll or focus group, funding it, selecting the research firm, constructing the questionnaire and gathering the data, analysing the data, interpreting the data, and disseminating those interpretations and data must be understood. Finally, I took it as a given that meaning and significance inhere in potentially every stage of the process, such as choice of data collection firm; sampling of respondents; sampling of the universe of potential questions; phrasing of the questions; analytic methods chosen and foregone; and attribution of meaning and significance to the results, especially in communications with the decision makers. Each of these parts of the process was deemed worthy of attention. The same can be said about each part of the public opinion shaping phenomenon, such as choice of advertising agency, choice of media, and choice of themes.

Propositions[1]

With appropriate tentativeness, a number of generalizations about government opinion research, as distinct from opinion research done for a political party or the mass media, can be drawn from our case studies. Of course, those generalizations are limited by the small number of case studies involved. Taken together, though, they comprise a model such as Blumer advocated. Before presenting them, it is useful to identify separately the building blocks—especially the dependent and independent variables[2]—found among those generalizations.

---

1. Some of the generalizations discussed below are taken from Ponting (2000b), which was based, in part, on a third and fourth case study involving the Government of Canada's polling and focus groups on (a) the Nisga'a Treaty and (b) the issue of an apology to Indigenous people in Canada.
2. I recognize that Blumer (1956) himself had major qualms, to say the least, about variables analysis. Not all of the generalizations offered in the present chapter take the form of the causal statements found in variables analysis.

The dependent variables, or matters to be explained in such a model, could be such phenomena as

- whether public opinion research will be conducted
- the uses to which the data are put
- who is included in the "inner circle" of decision makers
- which firm or consultant is selected to do the research
- size of the budget for the research
- deference to authority
- inclusiveness (versus secrecy and exclusivity)
- involvement of senior politicians or senior officials
- attention paid to sampling considerations
- sophistication of statistics used
- degree of simplification of findings in the research report or briefing
- "deviant" behaviour (e.g., leaking, gatekeeping in the distribution of data, failing to comply with regulations governing polling contracts and reporting)

Numerous independent variables, or causal factors, can also be identified in the propositions listed. The independent variables are

- urgency
- trust, distrust, and networks of trust
- the political stakes and symbolic importance of the issue
- degree of (un)certainty
- personal motivations
- power
- allure of polling data
- norms of professionalism and collegiality
- the imagined other (re: potential Freedom of Information requests)
- form (and norms) of accountability
- self-interest
- values of participants
- statistical sophistication of the client
- breadth of dissemination of questionnaire drafts and findings
- reference groups

We turn now to the generalizations themselves.

The Decision to Conduct and Resource the Research

The first proposition concerns the decision to sound public opinion at all. Whether polling is done, and how much, depends upon a variety of political, cultural, and idiosyncratic factors, including norms in the political culture, ministerial interest, and priorities of the government. The present research suggests that approvals for public opinion research and allocation of resources for that research are relatively easily obtained when the proposed research deals with issues that are politically or symbolically important to the government and uncertainty about public opinion prevails. Both the BC project and the Australian project were readily approved and generously resourced. However, other tapping of public opinion on Indigenous issues in Australia is rare because the uncertainty condition is not met—politicians believe that they already know what their constituents' sensitivities, priorities, and tolerances are on Indigenous issues.

Personal motivations—such as the desire to satisfy an information craving ("addiction"), the desire to protect a minister, a pollster's desire for another contract, the desire to leave a legacy, and the desire to augment one's own status, power, and influence—are significant factors in the decision of bureaucratic and political actors to conduct an opinion poll. For instance, the Premier's desire to leave a legacy (the Nisga'a Treaty), while not the prime motivation behind the British Columbia polling on Nisga'a, does appear to have been a consideration.

"Non-Rational" Considerations

Idiosyncratic personal considerations that transcend the rationality of law, politics, and economics enter the discourse surrounding public opinion research and its use. This emerged through advertising man Peter Lanyon in the Nisga'a case study and opinion researcher Irving Saulwick in Australia, as both were affected by the profound Indigenous spirituality that they encountered in their fieldwork. In the British Columbia situation, that spirituality and a near-religious zeal infused significant parts of the public discourse adopted for the advertising campaign.

One can readily imagine how such "non-rational" considerations could enter the discourse surrounding public opinion research on issues such as same-sex marriage, abortion, stem cell research, assisted suicide, terrorism or any other issue defined by claims-makers as having a strong moral dimension.

The Inherently Political Nature of Public Opinion Research

Public opinion research findings are a source of political power that can be exploited to the advantage of a given political actor, whether an individual, an organizational unit, a party, or a government. Therefore, rather than being delegated to middle level officials, public opinion research has a political overseer—Peter Vaughan (from the Department of the Prime Minister and Cabinet) in the Australian case study and Doug McArthur (Deputy Minister to the Premier) in the Nisga'a case study, and a ministerial staff member in the case of the Ottawa polling. This supervision ensures that the questionnaire construction and findings will be viewed through a political lens, regardless of the purposes of those who initiated the opinion research.

Different political actors bring their own personal agendas to the public opinion research undertaking, and public opinion research findings can be used in a wide variety of ways. For instance, at the macro level, they can be used to assess strategically the limits of what is politically possible, to influence another government or central agency, to help craft a public discourse and defuse opposition on the issue, or to influence the media. At the micro level, public opinion research findings can be used to confer prestige upon a political actor, to legitimate or vindicate an actor's arguments, to make others politically indebted to the actor, or to add momentum or staying power to one's work. To cite specific examples, John Heaney maintained that polling data eventually vindicated his arguments about the type of advertising the government should be doing on the Treaty. In Australia, the leaking of the Saulwick focus group findings may have placed some in the Prime Minister's office in the debt of the leaker or even demonstrated the loyalty of the leaker to the governing party. In Ottawa, departmental officials sought to influence the briefing of the minister when they thought that, if the explosive focus group findings were allowed to "trump" the more favourable survey findings, the hard work of their departmental colleagues on negotiating the Nisga'a Treaty might be for naught.

Mystique, Allure, and Urgency

Given the potential value and uses of public opinion data, and their ability to dissipate uncertainty, these data are in high demand. Indeed, public opinion data sometimes carry a certain mystique or allure among political insiders to the point where polling is said by some of them to be like an addiction or a narcotic —the "crack cocaine" of politicians in the words of interviewees in British Columbia and Ottawa. In the words of another British Columbia political administrator, "the more you do it [polling], the more you want it." In Australia, polling is widely used by politicians, but the allure of it is less noticeable, perhaps because of scandals over "push-polling."

To be without public opinion data is to be at a disadvantage in macro and/or micro politics. In British Columbia, McArthur received daily briefings on the results of the rolling polls, and in Australia, the Prime Minister's office let it be known clearly and forcefully that the Prime Minister himself wanted the data from the Newspoll survey.

In public opinion research, urgency is the norm. A corollary to this is that public opinion data have a short "shelf life." That is, the interest of politicians and bureaucrats is inversely proportional to the age of the data. As one Ottawa interviewee observed, "Two weeks after a poll is done, it's old news."

The ability to inject an historical perspective on public opinion data is rare and highly valued, which contributed to the influence that Doug McArthur (from his Yukon and Saskatchewan days) and Irving Saulwick (from his past focus group research) had in their respective projects. This principle is also applicable to the selection of consultants and to the selection of the firm to do the data collecting. It should be noted, though, that the greater the circulation of elites and the greater the staff cutbacks, the narrower will be the government's in-house historical horizons on public opinion.

Construction of the Questionnaire

The birth of a public opinion polling questionnaire is a social, team-like process wherein collegiality is the norm, and the exercise of blatant power is extremely rare, but not absent. That is, questionnaire construction is an arena for the exercise of power, as Peter Vaughan showed; however, as Doug McArthur emphasized, it is even more an arena for the exercise of influence. Behaviour in that arena will exhibit a mix of competitive collegial accountability and deference to authority, whether that authority is based on formal position or years of experience. Deference to authority will be muted and elastic (uneven). Among senior political administrators, the bald exercise of formal authority will be tempered by norms of professional collegiality. This is illustrated by Peter Vaughan's lack of insistence that his views prevail on some questions of lower priority to him and on the issue of the mail-out survey being dropped from the research design.

Construction of a proper questionnaire is painstaking work. Political actors who normally concern themselves with "the big picture" are willing to devote in-depth attention to the minutiae of questionnaire construction. This is illustrated by the interest taken in the Nisga'a questionnaires by Premier Clark and his Deputy Minister Doug McArthur, by the detailed notes written by Peter Vaughan on drafts of the Newspoll questionnaire, and by Australian pollster John Davis's comments about never having spent so much time agonizing over every word and every question in a questionnaire. Clearly, political actors are conscious of potential allegations of bias. Furthermore, they recognize the value of public opinion data generated by a carefully constructed questionnaire, and they are willing to make an investment of time in anticipation of reaping political rewards or avoiding political costs. Ironically, though, for projects with such high political stakes, scant resources are invested in pre-testing the questionnaire.

Given the close political scrutiny exercised during the questionnaire construction phase and the accountability created by the fact that results (with questions) are made available to the key political insiders who were involved in the questionnaire construction, there is little opportunity for deviance or disobedience in the questionnaire construction phase.

Sampling and Statistics

Sampling considerations are usually not the concern of political administrators. Noteworthy exceptions involve situations in which they wish to over-sample in population sectors that are of particular political salience and situations in which they wish to pre-empt or "trump" opponents and other potential critics. Arguments about sampling adequacy or representativeness are a resource that will be deployed by protagonists, either internally in advance or by external critics after the fact. At the extreme, such arguments call into question the very validity of the findings. Thus, sampling arguments are a tool in polling "wars" and an instrument for social control. With apologies for alliteration, we can say that sampling adequacy is an important part of the public persona of detached professionalism that protagonists project during political struggles.

The logic and discourse of mathematics and statistics are generally unwelcome in the policy community dealing with public opinion on Indigenous issues. Thus, appropriate opportunities for their use are usually foregone. This was found in Australia, British Columbia, and Ottawa. The statistics used to capture and assess the meaning and importance of the data are usually fairly rudimentary, such that the discourse of reporting public opinion research utilizes metaphors of unknown accuracy without subjecting them to verification. Causal analysis is rarely undertaken, even when it would contribute positively to the attainment of the research objectives. Opinion researchers do not expect ministers to be conversant with even moderately advanced statistics such as regression analysis and do not want to risk confusing the ministers or driving the cost of the research out of reach of the client's budget. Furthermore, to tread onto statistical terrain is to invite questions with answers that could be embarrassing (e.g., with regard to the small amount of variance explained) or that otherwise could undermine the mystique-based authority that pollsters have in the mind of some users of their data. The "emperor" (pollster) could be revealed to have no clothes, so to speak. Hence, pollsters are reluctant to take statistical analysis beyond simple cross-tabulations (with no controls) and segmentation analysis that identifies putatively discernible sectors of the population to which different political messages could be pitched. Significantly, notwithstanding their own doubts about the validity of segmentation methodology, some pollsters engage in segmentation analysis merely because it is in vogue, and the client wants it.

Interpreting the Data: Handling Nuance, Ambiguity, Contradiction, and Caveat

Ambiguity, contradiction, and caveat are common in public opinion data, especially on Indigenous issues. The more sophisticated the client is, the more comfortable the pollster will feel in presenting such "messiness." Increasingly, those who reach the lofty perch of political insider status do have such sophistication. Therefore, pollsters are prepared to show them the complexities of the data and, in both countries, have even adopted the metaphor of "drilling down" to describe an aspect of the statistical analysis involved in explicating complexity.

However, for ministerial briefings, simplification is a guiding virtue in narratives about public opinion. Thus, for ministers, opinion researchers are more likely to develop what might be called a "story line," which captures the gist of the findings and to which the researchers assimilate findings. Such a story line is an important form of interpretive filtering that affects the portrayal of public opinion received by ministerial decision makers. This form of filtering poses a danger, in that a pollster can become known for a particular theory of public opinion on Indigenous issues and may be reluctant to jettison that theory when the data so warrant.

In contrast to pollsters, focus group researchers thrive on nuance, ambiguity, contradiction, and caveat. It would be an exaggeration to say that those features of opinion are the raison d'être of qualitative researchers. However, those features of opinion do advance the self-interest of the qualitative researcher, for they demonstrate the need for his or her services and the advantage of qualitative over quantitative (polling) methodology.

Functions and Uses of Public Opinion Research

Public opinion data can serve many different functions. The democratic control model of public opinion (Lippman, 1925), rooted in a rather unflattering, nineteenth-century view of the mass public as irrational, sees public opinion as needing to be controlled. This model views polling as a means of increasing government autonomy from the mass public. Mills (1986, p. 48), quoting Benjamin Ginsberg (1982), refers to this social control, or domesticating, function of public opinion polling: "Polling renders public opinion less dangerous, less disruptive, more permissive, and more amenable to Government control." Instead of being a source of spontaneous outbursts of behaviour, public opinion has been channelled by polling into regular, subsidized expressions of attitude, notes Mills. In his words, polling forces the public to "telegraph its punches," which allows government to detect and deflect public criticism. Of course, using public opinion data for advertising aimed at persuading members of the public in a certain direction, as happened on the Nisga'a Treaty project, is an extreme case of what Mills and Ginsberg had in mind. This is using public opinion research in the service of legitimating government policy, by shaping the terms on which the public discourse on government policy is conducted. The use of public opinion research to shape the phraseology of the Canadian federal government's apology to aboriginal people served a similar, albeit perhaps more subtle, legitimating function.

The Council for Aboriginal Reconciliation's polling was also an instance of the general phenomenon of using polling to influence public opinion. However, rather than seeking to legitimate existing government policy, the Council was prepared to have that research shake up public opinion and bring pressure to bear on the government. More specifically, although the Council's public opinion research was intended (in part) to hold up a mirror to the nation so as to allow Australians to see themselves, it was not intended to be merely a passive mirror. Rather, as one interviewee (#1610) noted, that mirror itself was to become "an element of the equation."

Public opinion data also allow a government to bring its policies more in line with the pre-existing general will, although for reasons of ideology, financial cost, or principle, governments may resist such realignment. For instance, early in the existence of the Council for Aboriginal Reconciliation, Council members let it be known publicly that they would be informed by, but not driven by, public opinion on the reconciliation issue. For its part, the government of British Columbia steadfastly refused to hold a referendum on the Nisga'a Treaty, even though public opinion favoured such a referendum.

Public Opinion Processing as Social Activity

Our case studies also reveal that the social interactions through which even professionals grapple with the collection and use of public opinion data, and the shaping of public opinion, take on an emergent importance of their own. Otherwise stated, collecting and using public opinion data, and especially using it in an attempt to influence public opinion, are inherently sociological phenomena in which social processes like presentation of self, competition, status striving, role negotiation, exercise of power, and building of esprit de corps emerge. These sociological processes can be very consequential in determining the direction that a given public opinion project takes. The Nisga'a Treaty project is replete with examples. Among them are the near religious fervour that developed among many on the project and the loyalty that that fervour instilled, Peter Lanyon's captivation by Nisga'a spirituality and the reflection of that in his advertisements, and the near charismatic authority that Shawn Thomas exercised over some co-workers. In the reconciliation situation in Australia, examples would include the corrosive effects that the various leaks had on trust, with consequent effects on the distribution of subsequently acquired data.

The inherently sociological nature of public opinion research is also manifested in the influence of imagined others. That is, participants in questionnaire construction sometimes allow the content of the questionnaire to be influenced by others whom they believe could conceivably submit a request for the questionnaire under Freedom of Information legislation. This was especially true in the Ottawa case studies and will probably be more common in Australia as a result of the embarrassment arising from documents released under Senator Faulkner's Freedom of Information request. Ottawa interviewees also alluded to the fact that, by virtue of being included in the random sample, political opponents of the government could become aware of the research and ask questions about who is conducting such research. Imagined others also enter into sampling considerations in a minor way. That is, opinion research firms often screen eligible respondents with a question asking whether anyone in the family works for a polling firm. Such persons are excluded from the sample, with the result that the questionnaire is not exposed to critique and attack from commercial rivals of the polling firm.

Secrecy, Leaks, Accountability, and Trust

Public opinion polling is usually conducted in relative secrecy. Indeed, secrecy is ubiquitous, even where Freedom of Information legislation is in place. To allow the existence of government polling on symbolically important issues to become public knowledge is to invite criticism from political opponents, despite the fact that the opponents would probably be polling on the issue themselves if they were in office. Such criticism reached a crescendo in both the British Columbia and the Australia case studies.

Leaks, "gatekeeping" (selective filtering) in the distribution of data, and trust are all of major importance. Gatekeeping in the dissemination of the results to internal audiences is rendered difficult by audience members' awareness of the questionnaire content. However, where trust has been significantly compromised among insiders, such as by leaks, gatekeeping in dissemination of results is more likely, as happened in Australia.

With regard to leaks, it is one thing for a decision maker to know the main features of public opinion on an issue. However, it can be quite another matter altogether for that decision maker to be cognizant of the fact that the public is aware that she or he knows, which is what happens when leaked results are made public in the press. For instance, it may be more difficult to resist a certain line of action on an issue that has strong moral overtones (e.g., issuing an apology to Indigenous people or holding a referendum on the Nisga'a Treaty) if the public opinion results are leaked and are at odds with the government's proclivities.

Among senior political administrators dealing with public opinion research, loyalty and accountability to colleagues (Campbell & Szablowski, 1979) are more durable than accountability to bureaucratic and statutory norms governing public release of reports. For instance, in the Ottawa case studies, the Department of Indian Affairs and Northern Development was lax about meeting the requirement that copies of survey research reports be filed with the Department of Public Works and Government Services. In Australia, if the leaker(s) of the Saulwick report included one or more political administrators (and I emphasize the word "if"), the foregoing proposition might explain the willingness of the leaker(s) to violate their oath of office. The key, of course, is to identify which among several potential reference groups is the reference group to whom that loyalty and accountability are felt.

Trust and distrust emerged as a leitmotif in our case studies. Participants in the generation and processing of public opinion data must pass informal screening tests of trustworthiness and expertise. Informal social networks based on leisure (especially in the Ottawa case study) and past employment provide evidence of such trustworthiness and expertise. The importance of past employment was particularly evident in the British Columbia case study, where "old boy" networks were prominent.

Trust, based both on respect for experience and on confidence in technical ability, lies at the root of the influence of the pollsters and qualitative researchers at the questionnaire formulation stage in all my case studies. Trust based on those same qualities and on shared values enabled Premier Clark to delegate lead responsibility on the Nisga'a project to his Deputy Minister. In Australia, the trust of some members of the Council had to be re-won by staff members after Saulwick's focus group results were leaked. In addition, trust between the secretariat and the larger DPMC was compromised by the leaks and by the failure of Minister Herron's office to take the Council into its confidence before formulating and releasing the government's response to the "stolen generations" report. The earlier leaking of the *Draft Document for Reconciliation* also contributed to distrust. Now, the fact that trust was compromised in the three-cornered relationship between the Council, the secretariat, and the DPMC was a significant factor that affected the processing of public opinion from early in the polling phase. This compromised trust was one of the features that differentiated the Australian case from the Canadian case studies.

Final Thoughts

This book has provided some sociological insights into the "backstage" behaviour of political actors engaged in historic, high stakes efforts to realign relations between Indigenous peoples and the larger Australian and British Columbian society. In both cases, key players deemed it necessary to have a comprehensive, systematic, detailed, and nuanced understanding of public opinion in the larger non-Indigenous society (and in the Australian case, to some degree in the Indigenous population, too). New accommodations, in the form of a precedent-setting treaty, were up for ratification in British Columbia, while the groundwork for new accommodations was being prepared by the Council for Aboriginal Reconciliation in Australia. In both cases, the focal project was vigorously contested. In both cases, the First Minister was drawn in, albeit in contrasting roles. Premier Clark became a champion of the project and made it his government's highest priority for several months. Conversely, Prime Minister Howard professed support for reconciliation, but he and his government undermined it in important ways, such as the refusal to offer an apology to Indigenous peoples, the response to the "stolen generations" report, The Native Title Amendment Act, and fear mongering over the possibility of liability for Indigenous claims to compensation. Both projects stand out in the respective countries' history. Indeed, the uniqueness of the situations dictates that we be cautious with the empirical generalizations issuing from the research, for these were not typical exercises in government collection of public opinion data.

Blumer's exhortation that academics should study public opinion "by working backwards instead of by working forward" has proven useful in the present research. Rather than accepting public opinion research findings without question, in these case studies, we have come to see those findings (and the uses to which they are put) as products of socio-political dynamics involving the micro-politics of government offices and other forms of social interaction encompassing presentation of self, role negotiation, etc. Indeed, the very essence of public opinion research—namely, the determination of what questions do and do not get asked—is shaped by these sociological and political phenomena. Equally important, the conferral of meaning upon the findings obtained and the determination of who will be privileged in that meaning-conferral task (e.g., leakers versus project managers versus elected or appointed officials), are also very much determined by socio-political dynamics. This, too, can become contested terrain: as the Council for Aboriginal Reconciliation was told after the leak of the Saulwick report, "If you don't manage the release of the data, someone else will manage it for you."

The propositions presented earlier in this chapter can serve as one among several possible guides for conducting future research in the spirit of Blumer's exhortation. Here are examples of other questions that might engage researchers operating in the Blumerian spirit:

- What distinguishes the circumstances in which push-polling (inclusion of intentionally biased questions to achieve a preferred result) is used from circumstances in which it is eschewed? What are the long-term consequences of push-polling for those team members who acquiesced in it?
- What moral rationalizations are used to justify push-polling?
- When the results of the survey and the results of the focus groups are contradictory, what factors determine which will prevail?
- What is the moral and political calculus of leakers, and can typologies of leakers be formed?
- How do pollsters respond to generic challenges to the reliability and validity of their work (e.g., re-defining the concept of "participation rate" in the face of declining participation rates in telephone surveys)? How do pollsters maintain the authority and mystique surrounding their expertise?
- How is the processing of public opinion data in low priority issue areas different from that in high priority issue areas?
- What are the consequences of routinization within the polling industry?

The above are just a few research questions that have presented themselves in the course of the case studies reported in this book. It is evident that heeding Blumer's call can result in an enhanced understanding of some important historical events from a "behind the scenes" perspective, and it can also enhance our understanding of public opinion gathering (and use) as an intricate and complex sociological enterprise having highly contingent outcomes.

In which case, Australia or British Columbia, were democratic ideals better served? In the Foreword, I noted that this book is situated within the debate on the essence of democratic politics. In particular, my research project was surrounded by the issue of whether government should be responsive to public opinion and the issue of whether it is appropriate in a democracy for government to be proactive in seeking to lead and shape that public opinion. In the Australia case study, we saw an instance of the government refusing to lead—refusing to get out in front of public opinion to "bring it along"—because existing public opinion was consistent with the Prime Minister's own views. In the British Columbia case, we saw a politically desperate, fiercely determined, and intensely combative First Minister who experienced a political awakening and a "moral conversion" that moved him to throw himself into a public opinion leadership role with a vengeance. Unlike Prime Minister Howard, Premier Clark fully recognized the combined importance of the symbolic and the practical elements in the solution to the problem of incorporating Indigenous people as full members of society. Clark's team fully exploited (some would say "manipulated") the symbolic resources at its disposal. To accomplish the job of "selling" the Treaty to British Columbians, Clark inspired his team to what many experienced as "a higher calling" and provided the requisite instrumental resources, exhortative might, and symbolic leadership. Howard chose none of these as he manoeuvered within the confines of existing public opinion. Which approach shows more respect for democratic values, I leave for readers to decide. However, a propos of the issue, I give the final word in this space to an anonymous Australian interviewee who noted,

> If the Prime Minister had started with a different approach, the very people he's pointing to now [as constraining him] would have a different opinion.

Postscript: The Impact of the Nisga'a Treaty in Northwestern British Columbia

Debate on the Nisga'a Treaty included much escalated rhetoric, including dire economic predictions. In that context, it is worth noting that in the northwestern British Columbia community of Terrace, described by one observer as "the hotbed of protest against the Treaty," an accommodation between the town and the Nisga'a has been reached since the Treaty was signed.

The Greater Terrace area (population 20,000 in the 2001 Census of Canada) is centred on the town of Terrace, about an hour's drive south of New Aiyansh. Statistic after statistic on the website of the Terrace Economic Development Authority[1] points to a very significant economic decline in Terrace during the late 1990s and on through the early years of this century. For instance, the population declined 4.6% from 1996 to 2001, business incorporations declined markedly (from 57 in 1998 to 40 in 2003), and a marked drop occurred in housing starts, the full-time employed labour force, and arrivals and departures at the regional airport. This recession should not be attributed to the signing of the Treaty. Instead, the United States's imposition of a 27% import duty on softwood lumber and the closing of the Skeena Cellulose mill (140 jobs) are key factors that affected the economic health of the region (Persson, 2005). The closing of a provincial jail in Terrace also contributed to the economic downturn.

Given this economic decline, perhaps it is not surprising that non-Native leaders in northwestern BC have embraced the Nisga'a and other aboriginal peoples of the area. For instance, the tourism section of the *Five Year Strategic Economic Plan* issued in March 2003 by the Terrace Economic Development Authority says, "Our region is blessed with diverse First Nation culture with different traditions and a whole host of arts and crafts which tourists would certainly demand" (p. 8). The plan attaches high priority to various joint efforts with First Nations in the region, including initiatives in forestry (p. 3) and tourism (p. 9). Similarly, acknowledging "a growing economic presence by native peoples" and the Nisga'a people's building of an economic base, an editorial (Link, 2005b) in the *Terrace Standard* advocates that Terrace city council establish a closer relationship with its neighbouring First Nation governments. The editorial goes on to say,

> The native economic fact will continue to grow as more and more development opportunities arise affecting the city and area. Native governments are now on a par with municipal ones (and in some

---

1. See <www.teda.ca/downloads.htm>.

cases, hold greater sway) when it comes to being involved in key decision making.

At the very least, Terrace city council should host quarterly sessions between it, other municipalities, and native governments to compare notes and hammer out common goals of benefit to all.

The same newspaper also published a very laudatory celebration (Zimmerman, 2005) of the ninetieth birthday of Frank Calder, the Nisga'a leader who was instrumental in the pressing of the Nisga'a land claim and the landmark 1973 Supreme Court of Canada decision on aboriginal rights.

This new orientation toward the Nisga'a and other First Nations in British Columbia is prudent in light of their growing economic importance. For instance, the Nisga'a signed an agreement with the Government of British Columbia to involve the Nisga'a in potential offshore oil and gas development (if the federal and provincial governments lift their moratoria on offshore development), and both parties look to sign a similar agreement for land-based oil and gas development (Link, 2005a). A Nisga'a share of scores of billions of dollars is at stake here. Nisga'a Lisims Government President Nelson Leeson was quoted in the same article as saying "We want to do business." Other ways in which the northwestern BC regional economy was stimulated in the early years after the Treaty came into effect include increased spending by Nisga'a members in Terrace stores, the investment of tens of millions of dollars for the building of new housing and infrastructure (e.g., museum, government buildings, water and sewer lines) in the Nisga'a Territory, the injection of over $78 million in provincial highway construction, the investment of half of Nisga'a revenues under the Treaty (after payments on loans incurred during the Treaty negotiations) to generate future income, and the fostering of Nisga'a owned business ventures through Nisga'a funded loans (Bennett, 2002; Nagel, 2004). In 2005, the Nisga'a even entered discussions with an American investor who had purchased an abandoned mining town 40 kilometres north of New Aiyansh. "He'd like to see us play a real pivotal role in opening up the area so the whole northwest benefits," Leeson was quoted as saying with reference to the Nisga'a interest in heli-skiing, fly fishing, and eco-tourism (Nagel, 2005).

The about-face in the orientation of local non-Native leaders in the Nisga'a Treaty region has been accompanied by significant policy changes on the part of the provincial Liberals. Led by Gordon Campbell and Geoff Plant, they had opposed the Treaty strenuously in the pre- and early post-ratification stages. Campbell and Plant had even launched a lawsuit against the Treaty. The provincial Liberal government's new position, though, was applauded by First Nation leaders. As stated by Attorney-General Geoff Plant at a televised cabinet meeting in late 2002 (McInnis, 2002), the new policy abandoned the requirement that aboriginal rights be extinguished in treaty negotiations. It also declared the government's openness to negotiating aboriginal self-government, albeit as a power delegated to First Nations rather than as an inherent right. Whereas in the past the provincial

Liberals had held that certainty for investors was to be found in the wording of a treaty, the new policy was informed by the belief that real certainty will come only with an agreement with which all parties can work over time. In a letter he wrote in 2003, Plant went so far as to identify treaty settlements as a priority of the government:

> Negotiated settlements with First Nations ... represent an opportunity to achieve certainty over lands and resources in the region—an opportunity that our government has identified as a priority so that we can attract investment and create more economic stability in BC.

By 2004, Plant, like the Clark government's pro-Nisga'a Treaty campaign, was promoting treaty negotiations as creating "a platform of certainty" (Todd, 2004). Relations with First Nations, which had decidedly soured with the Liberals' provincial referendum on treaty negotiations, had begun to show marked improvement.[2] Treaty negotiations with First Nations regained momentum with the reaching of Agreements-in-Principle with the Snuneymexw First Nation (located adjacent to Nanaimo on Vancouver Island), the Lheidli T'enneh Band (near Prince George), the Sliammon First Nation (near Powell River) and others. In a move of poignant irony, the Liberal government embarked upon a sales job of its own to extol to British Columbians the benefits of Agreements-in-Principle reached with First Nations.

---

2. For a listing of BC treaty negotiations at an advanced stage and a thumbnail sketch of each one, see the website of the British Columbia Ministry of Aboriginal Relations and Reconciliation: <www.gov.bc.ca>.

Appendix 1: Selected Provisions of the Nisga'a Treaty

Land, Compensation, and Fiscal Transfers

- Recognition of Nisga'a title (rather than Crown title) to about 1,992 square kilometres of land in the lower Nass Valley of BC. These lands will not include lands subject to agricultural leases or wood lot licences or lands to which title is held in fee simple by third parties.
- Existing third party legal interests on Nisga'a lands will continue or be re-issued on their current terms.
- Land owned by the Nisga'a will not be considered Indian reserves under the Indian Act. Title will be held in fee simple by the Nisga'a.
- Financial compensation in the amount of $190 million, paid in instalments over 15 years, plus on-going funding (to be reduced over time in accordance with the Nisga'a Government's increased ability to raise its own revenues) for government services.
- Funding in the amount of $11.5 million to enable the Nisga'a Lisims Government to increase its capacity (vessels and licences) to participate in the commercial fishery.
- Funding in the amount of $10 million contributed by Canada and $3 million contributed by the Nisga'a for the establishment of the Lisims Fisheries Conservation Trust. The mandate of the Trust includes promoting the conservation and protection of Nass area fish species, facilitation of sustainable management of the fisheries, and other purposes.

Aboriginal Rights (in Canada)

- The Treaty is a full and final settlement of Nisga'a aboriginal rights and land claim and exhaustively sets out Nisga'a aboriginal rights under Section 35 of *The Constitution Act, 1982.*
- The Nisga'a agree to relinquish any aboriginal rights that are not set out in the Treaty, including aboriginal title and any aboriginal rights in the larger area included in the Nisga'a land claim.

Jurisdiction and Powers of the Nisga'a Central Government

- The Nisga'a will be governed locally by the Nisga'a Lisims Government (central government) and four Nisga'a Village Governments.
- Most Nisga'a laws, except traffic laws, will apply only to Nisga'a citizens. The Nisga'a Government must consult with non-Nisga'a residents of Nisga'a lands about decisions that significantly and directly affect them and permit them to participate in Nisga'a bodies that directly and significantly affect them. Such participation must include the right to make presentations, vote, seek election or appointment, and have the same means of appeal as Nisga'a citizens.
- The Nisga'a Lisims Government has legislative jurisdiction over

• Nisga'a citizenship	• public order, peace, and safety
• Nisga'a language and culture	• employment
• child custody and adoption	• education
• solemnization of marriages	• traffic and transportation
• child and family, social, and health services	• Nisga'a property in Nisga'a lands
• environmental assessment and protection, if Nisga'a standards meet or exceed federal and provincial standards	• In addition, it has the power to make laws required to carry out its responsibilities (e.g., forestry, fishing) under the Treaty.

Taxation
- The Nisga'a Lisims Government has the power to tax Nisga'a citizens on Nisga'a lands.
- The *Indian Act* exemption from taxation on-reserve is eliminated after a transitional period of eight years for transaction (e.g., sales) taxes and twelve years for other (e.g., income) taxes.
- Nisga'a governments will be treated in the same way as other BC municipalities for tax purposes.
- Nisga'a government corporations, operating solely on Nisga'a lands, will be exempt from federal and provincial income taxes.

Administration of Justice
- The Nisga'a may establish a Nisga'a Court to adjudicate prosecutions and civil disputes arising under Nisga'a laws and to review the administrative decisions of Nisga'a public bodies.
- In proceedings where the accused could face imprisonment under Nisga'a law, (s)he may elect to be tried instead in the Provincial Court of BC.
- Decisions of the Nisga'a Court may be appealed to the Supreme Court of BC on the same basis as decisions made by the Provincial Court of BC.
- Subject to provincial approval, the Nisga'a may establish a Nisga'a Police Service to provide policing within Nisga'a lands. It will have the full range of police responsibilities and authority to enforce Nisga'a, provincial, and federal laws, including the *Criminal Code of Canada*.

Cultural Artefacts and Heritage
- Return of numerous specified Nisga'a artefacts to the Nisga'a from the Royal BC Museum and the Canadian Museum of Civilization and sharing of numerous specified Nisga'a artefacts with those museums.
- Thirty-nine place names, Indian reserves, or key geographic features (e.g., rivers, creeks, villages, and a mountain) to be officially renamed with Nisga'a names.
- Protection of five Nisga'a sites to be designated as provincial heritage sites.

Natural Resources, Marine Species, and Wildlife
- Nisga'a ownership of all mineral and forest resources on or under Nisga'a lands. Following a five-year transition period, the Nisga'a will manage forestry on Nisga'a lands.
- Nisga'a entitlement to a guaranteed share of the harvest of salmon and an allocation of other marine and wildlife species (e.g., shellfish, aquatic plants, moose, grizzly bear, mountain goat), subject to conservation measures.
- Nisga'a entitlement to trade or barter wildlife and migratory birds among themselves or with other aboriginal people.
- Nisga'a entitlement to sell their salmon commercially and to catch steelhead only for domestic (non-commercial) purposes.
- Commitment by the provincial government to approve the Nisga'a purchase of forest tenure(s) outside Nisga'a lands with an allowable cut of up to 150,000 cubic metres of timber, subject to the *Forest Act*.
- Guarantees of a volume of flow in the Nass River for Nisga'a domestic, industrial, and agricultural uses.
- BC will consult with the Nisga'a Nation about applications for water licences involving streams wholly or partially within Nisga'a lands.
- The committee that advises the provincial minister on wildlife management will have equal representation from the Nisga'a and the Province, and one representative from Canada.
- The committee that advises the Minister on fisheries management will have two representatives from each of BC, Canada, and the Nisga'a.
- The federal and provincial governments retain responsibility for conservation and management of the fisheries and fish habitat. The Nisga'a Lisims Government may make laws to manage the Nisga'a fish harvest if such laws are consistent with the Nisga'a Annual Fishing

Plan, which itself is subject to review by a Joint Fisheries Management Committee and the approval of the Minister.

Restrictions on the Nisga'a
- The Nisga'a are prohibited from establishing large-scale fish processing plants within 8 years of the Treaty coming into effect.
- The Nisga'a are prohibited from establishing any primary timber processing facility within 12 years of the Treaty coming into effect.

Applicability of Federal and Provincial Laws
- *The Canadian Charter of Rights and Freedoms* will apply to the Nisga'a Government and its institutions.
- Federal and provincial laws, such as the *Criminal Code of Canada*, will continue to apply to Nisga'a citizens and others on Nisga'a lands.
- In the event of any inconsistency or conflict between the Treaty and any federal or provincial law, the Treaty will prevail to the extent of the inconsistency or conflict.
- The Nisga'a remain eligible for federal or provincial programs for aboriginal people.
- The *Indian Act* will cease to have applicability to the Nisga'a, except in determining whether an individual is an "Indian."
- The Treaty (see Sec. 7 and 58) explicitly states that it does *not alter the Constitution of Canada*.

Source: Indian & Northern Affairs Canada (n.d.).

Appendix 2: Chronology of British Columbia Events

1887 February: Nisga'a land claim launched as Nisga'a chiefs travel to Victoria to demand recognition of title, negotiation of treaties, and self-government.

1913 Nisga'a send a petition to the Privy Council in England seeking to resolve the land question.

1927 Federal *Indian Act* amended to make illegal both land claims organizing and fund-raising for land claims.

1951 Above provisions of *Indian Act* repealed.

1968 Nisga'a Tribal Council initiates litigation (known as the Calder case, after Nisga'a chief Frank Calder) in BC Supreme Court on the land question.

1973 January: Supreme Court of Canada decision on the Nisga'a claim (*Calder* case). Court is split 3–3, but deciding vote is cast against the Nisga'a on the grounds of the technicality that the plaintiffs had not sought the Crown's permission to sue the Crown.

August 8: Trudeau government introduces Comprehensive Land Claims Policy.

1976 January 12: Negotiations open on the Nisga'a claim.

1989 Canada and the Nisga'a Tribal Council sign a bilateral framework agreement that sets out the scope, process, and topics for negotiations.

1990 August 9: Social Credit Premier William Vander Zalm announces that BC will recognize aboriginal rights and abandon its policy of refusing to negotiate land claims.

1991 October 7: NDP government elected under leader Mike Harcourt, with 40.7% of the popular vote and 51 of 75 seats.

1992 September 21: Premier Harcourt and Prime Minister Mulroney sign agreement committing them to negotiate all land claims in BC by 2000.

"Bingogate" scandal erupts.

1994 June 29: Premier Mike Harcourt and Employment and Investment Minister Glen Clark (responsible for BC Ferries) announce the construction of three catamaran-style, high-speed ferries for the Nanaimo-Horseshoe Bay run and say that they will cost $70 million each and be in the water by early 1996. The government says that the project will revitalize BC's ship-building industry as the vessels will be sold around the world.

December 12: Liberal MLA releases letter to Clark saying fast ferries project is "fraught with unacceptable risk."

1995 May 3: Road blockade by members of Upper Nicola Band begins at Douglas Lake Ranch.

June 6: End of road blockade at Douglas Lake Ranch.

June: Land dispute begins at Gustafsen Lake, BC, with occupation after sundance.

September 17: End of four week armed stand-off at Gustafsen Lake.

November 15: Premier Mike Harcourt announces his resignation as Premier and as NDP leader, although he personally was not implicated in the "Bingogate" (Nanaimo Commonwealth Holding Society) scandal.

1996 February 12: Negotiators announce they have reached an Agreement-in-Principle on the Nisga'a claim. It is initialled three days later.

February 18: Glen Clark wins NDP leadership campaign to become Premier.

March 22: Nisga'a Agreement-in-Principle is formally signed at New Aiyansh by Nisga'a Tribal Council President Joseph Gosnell, Sr. and for the provincial and federal governments by Ministers John Cashore and Ronald Irwin, respectively.

May 28: NDP is re-elected with a reduced majority of 39 seats and 39.5% of the popular vote, compared to Liberals' 33 seats and 41.8% of the popular vote. Three seats go to other parties.

July 6: NDP government admits the budget surplus forecasted during election campaign ("Fudge-it Budget") will actually be a deficit of as much as $235 million.

October 15: BC Auditor General announces that he will begin an investigation into the NDP government's budget forecasting, after media receive leaked documents showing Ministry of Finance had forewarned the government about the problems with the provincial budget.

December 11: Delgamuukw decision favouring aboriginal rights in British Columbia announced by Supreme Court of Canada.

1998 January 2: Newspaper report quotes an engineer as saying BC Ferries' estimates for the cost and completion date of its first fast ferry are "a big joke." Engineer backs Liberal ferries critic's contention that the cost will increase to $100 million per ship.

April: John Heaney hired to lead the provincial government's Nisga'a polling and advertising campaign.

April 28: Eight focus groups on the Treaty conducted by Angus Reid Group in Vancouver, Prince George, Terrace, and Fraser Valley as negotiations on Final Agreement were concluding.

May 11–19: Baseline Wave I provincial government survey conducted on Nisga'a Treaty by Angus Reid.

June: Fast ferries' harshest critic, Progressive Democratic Alliance leader Gordon Wilson, calls for Auditor General to audit BC Ferry Corporation.

August 4: Nisga'a Treaty signed by Canada, British Columbia, and Nisga'a—Minister Jane Stewart, Premier Glen Clark, and Chief Joseph Gosnell, Sr.

August 19–21: Wave II of polling for provincial government's Nisga'a Treaty advertising campaign conducted.

August 4 or 7: First ads in advertising campaign appear.

September 21: Delivery of pamphlet on Treaty to every household in BC.

October 16: Fisheries Survival Coalition, Reform MP John Cummins, and others launch law suit against Nisga'a Treaty in BC Supreme Court.

October 19: Gordon Campbell (Leader of the BC Liberal Party) and Geoff Plant launch lawsuit challenging the constitutionality of the Nisga'a Treaty.

November 7: Treaty ratified by vote of the Nisga'a people. Supporters outnumber opponents by a ratio of about 3:1.

November 30: After a colourful Nisga'a ceremony, replete with the symbolic arrival of a Nisga'a canoe, provincial legislature (36th Parliament, 3rd Session) is recalled to deal with the Nisga'a Treaty enabling legislation entitled *The Nisga'a Final Agreement Act* (Bill 51).

November 30: CBC televises debate on Nisga'a Treaty by provincial party leaders Clark, Campbell, Vander Zalm, and Wilson. Green Party leader Parker is denied participation.

December 4: Lawsuit against the Treaty launched by BC Citizens First Coalition.

December 14: BC legislature adjourns for Christmas break.

1999 January 13: BC legislature reconvenes. Second reading given to *The Nisga'a Final Agreement Act*.

January 29: Gordon Wilson crosses floor of legislature and becomes Minister of Aboriginal Affairs and Minister responsible for BC Ferry Corp.

February 1: Legislature adjourns.

March 2: Premier Clark's home raided by RCMP. Criminal charges are subsequently laid, but Glen Clark is eventually exonerated in court.

March 29: BC legislature reconvenes.

April 22: After longest legislative debate (120 hours over 30 days) in BC history, Nisga'a Treaty enabling legislation passes in BC legislature by a vote of 39 to 32 (along strict party lines), after government imposes closure. Liberal Opposition walks out in protest against use of closure.

April 26: Nisga'a Treaty enabling legislation given royal assent and passed into law.

July: Explorer, the first of the fast ferries, goes into service.

August 21: Glen Clark announces his resignation as Premier.

October 28: Auditor General releases scathing report that is highly critical of the NDP government's handling of the fast ferries project. Total cost of the three ferries is now estimated to be $463 million, rather than the originally stipulated $210 million. In the report, Glen Clark is blamed for rushing the project.

December 13: Federal enabling legislation (Bill C-9) for Nisga'a Treaty passed by House of Commons on a vote of 217 to 48, as Liberals use closure to defeat Reform Party delaying tactics that had involved the introduction of a record 471 amendments requiring 42 hours and 34 minutes of debate and costing over $1 million in overtime pay for House of Commons staff.

2000 March 13: Deputy Premier Joy McPhail admits the fast ferries program is "a failed experiment" and says the government hopes to sell the three ships for about $40 million each. Two days later, Premier Dosanjh apologizes publicly for the fast ferries "huge mistake."

April 13: Nisga'a Treaty federal enabling legislation passed by Senate of Canada by a vote of 52–15 (13 abstentions) and is given royal assent and proclaimed into law that evening.

May 11: Nisga'a Treaty comes into effect. Nisga'a government holds its first meeting under the Treaty.

July 24: BC Supreme Court rules against Campbell and Plant in their lawsuit against the Nisga'a Treaty.

2001 May 16: BC Liberals win provincial election, in part on a platform of holding a referendum on the treaty-making process. NDP is reduced to holding two seats in legislature (21.6% of the popular vote), while Liberals, under leader Gordon Campbell, win 77 seats and 57.6% of the popular vote in the 79 seat legislature.

August: Premier Gordon Campbell and Geoff Plant withdraw their personal lawsuit against Nisga'a Treaty by foregoing appeal of July 2000 court ruling.

2002 May 15: Provincial mail-in referendum on treaty-making process ends with 35.8% participation rate. Questions and results are available from Elections BC at <www.elections.bc.ca/referendum/finalresults.pdf>.

Sources: Indian and Northern Affairs Canada (n.d.); Hill (2002, 2003); Lochead (2004); Rutherdale (2002); BC Archives (File GR-2964, Box 17), and miscellaneous newspaper accounts accessed electronically via Canadian Newsstand software.

Appendix 3: Opinion Research Conducted on Nisga'a Issue for BC Government or New Democratic Party

Report Date	Field Date	Type	Unweighted Sample	Firm	BC Archives Box & File # GR-2964	Description
not shown	1996	Survey & Focus Groups	800	unknown	not archived	Baseline at time AIP concluded
April 28/98	April 17/98	Focus Groups	8 groups	Angus Reid	Box 17, File 16	Vancouver, Prince George, Terrace, Fraser Valley. Informed survey questionnaire content.
May 26/98	May 11-19/98	Survey	900	Angus Reid	Box 17, File 17	Baseline: Wave I
August 17/98	c. August 11/98	Survey	800	Viewpoints	Box 17, File 18	3 dependent variables; 9 independent variables; chi-squared analysis. Client was New Democratic Party, not government.
August 19/98	c. August 16-18/98	Survey	600	Angus Reid	Box 17, File 19	Day 3 (N of 600 is 3-day cumulative total)
August 26/98	August 19-21/98	Survey	600	Angus Reid	Box 17, File 19&20	Wave II Executive Summary Report where May 1998 research is baseline.
undated	c. September 24-28/98	Survey	600	Angus Reid	Box 17, File 21	Wave III: Shows Aug. 24 & Sept. 28 breakouts
September /98	September 22-30/98	Survey (listened to radio ads)	150	McIntyre & Mustel	Box 17, File 22	Conducted in Burnaby and Langley. Included some ads that had not yet aired.

Report Date	Field Date	Type	Unweighted Sample	Firm	BC Archives Box & File # GR-2964	Description
October 13/98	early October /98	Survey	unknown	Angus Reid	not archived	Wave III. Referenced in tracking report of November 17.
November 17/98	Oct. 28-Nov. 1 /98	Survey	400	Angus Reid	Box 17, File 23	Wave I.a
	November 2-8 /98	Survey	400	Angus Reid	Box 17, File 23	Wave I.b
November 17/98	November 12-16 /98	Survey	700	Angus Reid	Box 17, File 23	Wave II

NOTE: Research conducted for the Party would not normally be sent to BC Archives. Thus, the record here is probably incomplete.

Appendix 4: Schedule of BC Government Newspaper and Magazine Advertisements on the Nisga'a Treaty

DAILY NEWSPAPERS	August 13 or 14, 1998			August 26 – September 1, 1998			September 9 – November 15, 1998 Maximum: Sept. 9, 11, 16, 23, Oct. 1, 5, 9, and Nov. 6 (or 7), 10		
	Columns	Lines	App*	Columns	Lines	App*	Columns	Lines	App*
Cranbrook Daily Townsman	5	150	1	5	150	1	7	200	9
Dawson Creek PRB News	5	150	1	5	150	1	7	200	9
Fort St. John Highway News	5	150	1	5	150	1	7	200	9
Kamloops Daily News	5	150	1	5	150	1	7	200	9
Kelowna Daily Courier	5	150	1	5	150	1	7	200	9
Kimberly Daily Bulletin	5	150	1	5	150	1	7	200	9
Nanaimo Daily News	5	150	1	5	150	1	7	200	9
Nelson Daily News	5	150	1	5	150	1	7	200	9
Okanagan Saturday			0			0	7	200	3
Penticton Herald	5	150	1	5	150	1	7	200	6
Port Alberni Valley Times	5	150	1	5	150	1	7	200	9
Prince George Citizen	5	150	1	5	150	1	7	200	9
Prince Rupert Daily News	5	150	1	5	150	1	7	200	9
Trail Times	5	150	1	5	150	1	7	200	9
Globe and Mail (BC Edition)	3	150	1	3	150	1	4	200	5
Vancouver Province							6	150	5
Vancouver Sun							7	200	5
Victoria Times-Colonist							7	200	5
Financial Post (BC Edition)							4	150	6
Cost	$6,268			$6,268			$154,729		

* Appearances

ETHNIC NEWSPAPERS	August 13 or 14, 1998			August 26 – September 1, 1998			September 9 – November 15, 1998 Maximum: Sept. 9, 11, 16, 23, Oct. 1, 5, 9, and Nov. 6 (or 7), 10		
	Columns	Lines	App*	Columns	Lines	App*	Columns	Lines	App*
Celtic: Celtic Connection							⅔ page = 6" x 10.25"		1
Chinese: Sing Tao (Cantonese†)							⅔ page = 8" x 14.25"		5
Ming Pao (Cantonese†)							⅔ page = 8" x 14.25"		5
World Journal (Mandarin†)							⅔ page = 8" x 14.25"		5
Dutch: The Windmill Herald							4	150	2
Filipino: Philippine Chronicle							⅔ page = 13" x 13"		3
Philippine Journal							⅔ page = 6.75" x 10.25"		3
Greek: Opinions							⅔ page = 6" x 12"		2
Hispanic: El Contacto Directo							⅔ page = 6.5" x 8.75"		5
Italian: L'Eco D'Italia†							4	150	5
Japanese: Vancouver Shinpo							4	150	5
Jewish: Jewish Western Bulletin							4	150	5
Korean: Vancouver Korean Press							⅔ page = 13" x 14"		5
Punjabi: The Indo-Canadian Voice							4	150	5
The Link							4	150	5
Indo-Canadian Times†							4	150	5
Indo-Canadian Phulwari†							4	150	1
Chardhi Kala†							⅔ page = 6.75" x 9.25"		5
Awaaz†							4	150	5
Guardian†							2.5	150	5
Russian: Vancouver & US Russian Nwsppr							⅔ page = 7.25" x 11.25"		2
SE Asian: Southeast Asia Post							⅔ page = 6.75" x 15"		3

† Translation

Publication				
Swedish: Swedish Press	Full page = 7.25" x 10"			1
Vietnamese: Vietnamese Times	⅔ page = 6" x 8"			5
Cost	$50,110			
ABORIGINAL PUBLICATIONS				
Ha-Shilth-Sa	⅔ page = 6.5" x 10.75"			3
Kahtou		168	4	1
Windspeaker (Canada)		150	4	1
Raven's Eye (BC Edition)		150	4	2
Aboriginal Times	Full page = 5" x 8"			1
Secwepemc News	⅔ page = 6.75" x 12"			1
First Nations Drum	⅔ Page = 7.5" x 11"			1
Cost	$9,289			
ALTERNATE PUBLICATIONS				
Monday Magazine		150	4	4
Vancouver Georgia Straight		150	3	4
Cost	$7,960			
CAMPUS PUBLICATIONS				
BCIT Link		140	4	2
Camosun College—The Nexus		150	4	2
Capilano College Courier		125	3	2
Douglas College Other Press		150	4	3
Langara College Gleaner		150	3	2
Malaspina College Navigator		150	3	2
Okanagan College Phoenix		125	3	2
Simon Fraser Peak		140	4	3
UBC Campus Times		150	4	3

	August 13 or 14, 1998			August 26 – September 1, 1998			September 9 – November 15, 1998 Maximum: Sept. 9, 11, 16, 23, Oct. 1, 5, 9, and Nov. 6 (or 7), 10		
	Columns	Lines	App*	Columns	Lines	App*	Columns	Lines	App*
CAMPUS PUBLICATIONS							⅔ page = 6" x 8.5"		
Ubyssey									3
UNBC Over the Edge							4	140	2
U of Victoria Martlet							4	150	3
Cost								$11,278	
COMMUNITY NEWSPAPERS									
Abbotsford News	3	150	1	3	100	1	5	200	9
Abbotsford-Mission Times	3	100	1	3	100	1	4	150	9
Agassiz Advance							4	150	7
Agassiz-Harrison Observer	3	100	1	3	100	1	4	150	6
Aldergrove Star	3	100	1	3	100	1	4	150	7
Armstrong Advertiser	3	100	1	3	100	1	4	150	7
Ashcroft, Cache Creek Journal	3	100	1	3	100	1	4	150	6
Barriere, N. Thompson Star/Journal	3	100	1	3	100	1	4	150	6
Bella Coola Valley, Coast Mtn News	3	100	1	3	100	1	4	150	4
Bowen Island Undercurrent	3	100	1	3	100	1	4	150	7
Burnaby/New West News Leader	3	100	1	3	100	1	4	150	9
Burnaby Now	3	100	1	3	100	1	4	150	9
Burns Lake, Lakes District News	3	100	1	3	100	1	4	150	7
Campbell River Courier-Islander	5	150	1	5	150	1	7	200	9
Campbell River Mirror	3	150	1	3	150	1	5	200	9
Campbell River, North Islander	5	100	1	5	100	1	6	150	7
Castlegar Sun	5	150	1	5	150	1	7	200	7
Chetwynd Echo	3	100	1	3	100	1	4	150	6

Chilliwack Progress	3	100	1	3	100	1	3	100	4	150	9
Chilliwack Times	3	100	1	3	100	1	3	100	4	150	8
Christine Lake News									2	144	4
Clearwater (Barriere) N. Thomps Tms	4	150	1	4	150	1	4	150	4	150	6
Colwood, Goldstream News Gazette	3	100	1	3	100	1	3	100	4	150	7
Comox Totem Times	3	100	1	3	100	1	3	100	4	150	7
Coquitlam Now	3	100	1	3	100	1	3	100	4	150	3
Coquitlam Tri-City News	3	100	1	3	100	1	3	100	4	150	9
Courteney, Comox Valley Record	3	100	1	3	100	1	3	100	4	150	9
Courtenay, Comox Valley Echo	5	150	1	5	150	1	5	150	7	200	9
Cranbrook East Kootenay Weekly	5	100	1	5	100	1	5	100	6	150	7
Cranbrook East Kootenay Advertiser	3	100	1	3	100	1	3	100	4	150	6
Creston Valley Advance	3	100	1	3	100	1	3	100	4	150	8
Dawson Creek Mirror	3	100	1	3	100	1	3	100	4	150	7
Delta Optimist	3	100	1	3	100	1	3	100	4	150	9
Duncan, The Citizen	5	100	1	5	100	1	5	100	6	150	9
Duncan, Cowichan News Leader									4	150	7
Duncan Pictorial	3	100	1	3	100	1	3	100	4	150	2
Elk Valley Extra (Fernie)	3	100	1	3	100	1	3	100	6	150	7
Enderby Commoner	3	100	1	3	100	1	3	100	4	150	7
Esquimalt News	3	100	1	3	100	1	3	100	4	150	7
Fernie Free Press	5	150	1	5	150	1	5	150	7	200	6
Fort Nelson News	3	150	1	3	150	1	3	150	7	200	7
Fort St. James Caledonia Courier	3	100	1	3	100	1	3	100	4	150	7
Fort St. John Northerner	3	100	1	3	100	1	3	100	4	150	6
Fort St. John, North Peace Express									4	150	7
Gabriola Sounder	3	100	1	3	100	1	3	100	4	150	3

COMMUNITY NEWSPAPERS	August 13 or 14, 1998			August 26 – September 1, 1998			September 9 – November 15, 1998 Maximum: Sept. 9, 11, 16, 23, Oct. 1, 5, 9, and Nov. 6 (or 7), 10		
	Columns	Lines	App*	Columns	Lines	App*	Columns	Lines	App*
Ganges Gulf Island Driftwood	3	100	1	3	100	1	4	150	7
Gibsons Coast Independent	3	100	1	3	100	1	4	150	6
Gold River, The Record	3	100	1	3	100	1	4	150	4
Golden News	3	100	1	3	100	1	4	150	7
Golden Star	3	100	1	3	100	1	4	150	7
Grand Forks Boundary Bulletin	3	100	1	3	100	1	4	150	6
Grand Forks Gazette	3	100	1	3	100	1	4	150	7
Greenwood, The Boundary Creek	3	100	1	3	100	1	4	150	6
Gulf Islands, Island Tides	3	100	1	3	100	1	4	150	4
Hope Standard	3	100	1	3	100	1	4	150	7
Houston Today	3	100	1	3	100	1	4	150	7
Invermere, Lk Windermere Valley Echo	3	100	1	3	100	1	4	150	7
Kaslo-Kootenay Lake Pennywise	3	135	1	3	135	1	3	135	6
Kamloops This Week	3	100	1	3	100	1	4	150	9
Kelowna Capital News	3	100	1	3	100	1	4	150	9
Keremeos, Gazette of the Similkameen	3	100	1	3	100	1			0
Kitimat, Northern Sentinel	3	100	1	3	100	1	4	150	7
Kitimat/Terrace Weekend Advertiser							4	150	7
Kootenay Weekly Express (Nelson)							4	150	4
Ladysmith-Chemainus Chronicle	3	100	1	3	100	1	4	150	6
Lake Cowichan Gazette							4	150	4
Lake Cowichan, The Lake News	5	100	1	5	100	1	6	150	7
Langley Advance News	3	100	1	3	100	1	4	150	9

Newspaper									
Langley Times	3	100	1	3	100	1	4	150	9
Lillooet Bridge River News	3	100	1	3	100	1	4	150	7
Mackenzie, The Times	3	100	1	3	100	1	4	150	6
Maple Ridge News	3	100	1	3	100	1	4	150	9
Maple Ridge Pitt Meadows Times	3	100	1	3	100	1	4	150	9
Merritt Herald	3	100	1	3	100	1	4	150	7
Merritt News	3	100	1	3	100	1	4	150	7
Merritt/Nicola Thompson Today	3	100	1	3	100	1	4	150	6
Mission, Fraser Valley Record	3	100	1	3	100	1	4	150	7
Nakusp Arrow Lake News	3	100	1	3	100	1	4	150	6
Nanaimo Bulletin	3	100	1	3	100	1	4	150	9
Nanaimo Harbour City Star	5	150	1	5	150	1	7	200	9
Nelson West Kootenay Weekender	3	100	1	3	100	1	4	150	7
New Denver Valley Voice	3	100	1	3	100	1	4	200	1
New Denver Valley Voice					100	1	4	150	2
New West, Royal City Record Now	3	100	1	3	100	1	4	150	9
North Shore News	3	100	1	3	100	1	4	150	9
Oak Bay News	3	100	1	3	100	1	4	150	6
Oliver Chronicle	3	150	1	3	150	1	4	150	7
Osoyoos Times	3	100	1	3	100	1	4	150	6
100 Mile House Free Press	3	100	1	3	100	1	4	150	7
Parksville-Qualicum News	3	100	1	3	100	1	4	150	9
Parksville Morning Sun	5	100	1	5	100	1	6	150	7
Peachland Signal	3	100	1	3	100	1	4	150	7
Pemberton Valley News	¼ page	1		¼ pg = 5.25" x 7.13"	1		10" x 12"	4

COMMUNITY NEWSPAPERS	August 13 or 14, 1998			August 26 – September 1, 1998			September 9 – November 15, 1998 Maximum: Sept. 9, 11, 16, 23, Oct. 1, 5, 9, and Nov. 6 (or 7), 10		
	Columns	Lines	App*	Columns	Lines	App*	Columns	Lines	App*
Penticton Western News (Tuesdays)	3	100	1	3	100	1	4	150	6
Penticton Western News (Fridays)							4	150	3
Port Hardy, North Island Gazette	3	100	1	3	100	1	4	150	7
Port Hardy, North Island Weekender	3	100	1	3	100	1	4	150	7
Powell River News	3	100	1	3	100	1	4	150	7
Powell River The Peak	3	100	1	3	100	1	4	150	7
Powell River Town Crier							4	150	7
Prince George Free Press	3	100	1	3	100	1	4	150	9
Prince George This Week	3	100	1	3	100	1	6	150	7
Prince Rupert This Week							4	150	7
Princeton Similkameen News Leader	3	100	1	3	100	1	4	150	7
Princeton Similkameen Spotlight	3	100	1	3	100	1	4	150	7
Queen Charlotte Islands Observer	2	100	1	2	100	1	3	140	7
Quesnel, Cariboo Observer	3	100	1	3	100	1	4	150	9
Revelstoke Times Review	3	100	1	3	100	1	4	150	7
Richmond News	3	100	1	3	100	1	4	150	9
Richmond Review	3	100	1	3	100	1	4	150	9
Salmon Arm Observer	4	150	1	4	150	1	5	200	7
Salmon Arm, Shuswap Market News	3	100	1	3	100	1	4	150	7
Salmon Arm, The Shuswap Sun	3	100	1	3	100	1	4	150	7
Salmon Arm Shoppers' Guide							4	150	6
Saanich News	3	100	1	3	100	1	4	150	7
Sechelt Express	3	100	1	3	100	1	4	150	7

Sicamous, Eagle Valley News	3	100	1	3	100	1	4	150	7
Sidney, Peninsula News Review	3	100	1	3	100	1	4	150	7
Smithers, The Interior News	4	150	1	4	150	1	5	200	7
Sooke News Mirror	3	100	1	3	100	1	4	150	7
Sparwood, The Elk Valley Miner	3	150	1	3	150	1	4	200	6
Squamish Chief	3	100	1	3	100	1	4	150	6
Stewart Signal							4	Full page = 8,5" x 11"	4
Summerland Review	3	100	1	3	100	1	4	150	7
Sunshine Coast Reporter (Gib & Sech)	3	100	1	3	100	1	4	150	6
Surrey City Now (All Zones)	3	100	1	3	100	1	4	150	9
Surrey N. Delta Leader	3	100	1	3	100	1	4	150	9
Terrace Standard	4	150	1	4	150	1	5	200	7
Terrace Times	3	100	1	3	100	1	4	150	7
Thompson Valley News (Clearwater)	3	100	1	3	100	1	4	150	7
Tofino, The Westerly News/Ucluelet	3	100	1	3	100	1	4	150	7
Tumbler Ridge Observer	3	100	1	3	100	1	4	150	7
Valemount, The Valley Sentinel	3	100	1	3	100	1	4	150	7
Vancouver Courier (Wednesdays)	3	100	1	3	100	1	4	150	7
Vancouver Courier (Sundays)							4	150	7
Vancouver Echo	3	100	1	3	100	1	4	150	7
Vanderhoof, Omineca Express-Bugle	3	100	1	3	100	1	4	150	7
Vernon Morning Star	3	100	1	3	100	1	4	150	9
Vernon Sun	3	100	1	3	100	1	4	150	9
Victoria News							4	150	7
Victoria, Greater Victoria Weekender	3	100	1	3	100	1	4	150	7
Westender (Vancouver)	3	100	1	3	100	1	4	150	2
West End Times (Vancouver)	3	100	1	3	100	1	4	150	7

	August 13 or 14, 1998			August 26 – September 1, 1998			September 9 – November 15, 1998 Maximum: Sept. 9, 11, 16, 23, Oct. 1, 5, 9, and Nov. 6 (or 7), 10		
COMMUNITY NEWSPAPERS	Columns	Lines	App*	Columns	Lines	App*	Columns	Lines	App*
Whistler, The Whistler Question	3	100	1	3	100	1	4	150	8
Whistler Pique	3	100	1	3	100	1	4	180	7
White Rock, The Peace Arch News	3	100	1	3	100	1	4	150	9
Williams Lake, The Tribune	4	150	1	4	150	1	5	200	9
Winfield, The Calendar	3	100	1	3	100	1	4	150	7
Vancouver E. Side Revue	3	100	1	3	100	1	4	150	3
Vancouver W. Side Revue	3	100	1	3	100	1	4	150	3
Cost	$34,092			$33,690			$502,276		
BUSINESS MAGAZINES									
Business in Vancouver							⅔ pg = 8 7/16" x 11 7/16 "		2
West Coast Fisherman							Full pg = 7.38" x 9.75"		1
Business Logger							Mag Pg = 8.5" x 11.5"		1
Journal of Commerce							Mag Pg = 8.5" x 11.5"		2
Sounding Board							Mag Pg = 8 3/16" x 10"		1
Cost							$10,290		

Appendix 5: Content of Nisga'a Treaty TV Ad Featuring David Suzuki

Length: 60 seconds
Background Music: Native singing accompanied by drumming

Spoken Text	Visual Image
I hope one day the Canadian people build a monument to the completion of this Treaty.	• tall Nisga'a totem pole, close-up and distal with forest and mountains in background.
And I want to be able to take my grandchildren to that monument, and I want to say to my grandchildren, "Look,	• Suzuki, upper body shot, against backdrop of foliage.
	• meadow with yellow flower waving in breeze.
those people, who lived on this land for thousands of years, who had vibrant rich lives and cultures,	• black and white drawing (photo?) of Nisga'a male in traditional attire, dissolve to bell, dissolve to close-up of Nisga'a child beside flower, dissolve to overhead view of two houses or cabins in a clearing in the forest; out of focus close-up of a carving then brought into focus; colourful Nisga'a mask worn by person.
they were decimated by disease, by the conquest of people from elsewhere.	• Suzuki, upper body shot, against backdrop of foliage.
They were treated terribly;	• Two children and bicycle outside doors of building with sign "The Salvation Army Citadel."
they suffered enormously.	• Child (approximately age 6) in front of building (needing paint) with Canadian flag painted on it.
But they knew the land mattered to them,	• Suzuki, upper body shot, against backdrop of foliage.
and they had patience and respect for themselves.	• Two Nisga'a women preparing food outside a rustic structure (a cabin?); close-up of child held by grandfather, resting her head on his shoulder, against out of focus forest background.
And they waited for over a hundred years.	• Suzuki gesturing, upper body shot, against backdrop of foliage.
And they negotiated openly, with respect,	• close-up of above black and white drawing of young Nisga'a adult male in traditional attire.
	• zooming in on flowing river with forest and cloudy sky.
	• distant Nisga'a adult, seemingly in gauze shirt, arms upraised as if in prayer, backlit by sun and sky, framed by forest with small waterfall and large tree in foreground.

with people who had taken their lands.	• Suzuki gesturing, upper body shot, against backdrop of foliage.
	• extreme close-up of part of a tree trunk.
And in the end, they gave up the vast bulk of the territory of their ancestors.	• distant scenic mountains, forest in foreground, blue sky.
	• Nisga'a man in traditional coat, framed by an evergreen branch.
And they completed generously, and honourably, this Treaty.	• Suzuki gesturing, upper body shot, against backdrop of foliage.
	• White lettering on black background: "The Nisga'a Treaty, 1-800-880-1022. British Columbia" and provincial coat of arms.

Source: www.peterlanyon.ca
Viewed July 26, 2004

Appendix 6: Two British Columbia Polling Questionnaires on the Nisga'a Treaty

August 19, 1998 Question Topic and Number	September 1998 Question Topic and Number (NOTE: This questionnaire did not contain any Q5 or Q6.)
1. Most important issue	1. Same as August 19, 1998 question
2. Awareness of Nisga'a Treaty and other issues	2. Similar, but dropped reference to other issues
3. Best thing about the Treaty	NOT ASKED
4. Worst thing about the Treaty	NOT ASKED
5. Nisga'a Treaty a step in right or wrong direction	7. Same
5A. Support or oppose Nisga'a Treaty	3. Same
	4. If "Don't Know," which way leaning
6. Likelihood of involvement in supportive letter-writing campaign	NOT ASKED
7. Likelihood of involvement in oppositional letter-writing campaign	NOT ASKED
8. Ever discussed Nisga'a Treaty with others	8. Same
9. If "Yes," discussion partners supportive or disapproving of Nisga'a Treaty	9. Same
10. Recall encountering Nisga'a Treaty in any of 7 places	10. Same, except "Newspapers" broken into two separate sources—"Newspaper reports" and "Newspaper advertising"
	11. What is the next step taken with the Treaty
11. Form own opinion on Treaty independently or based on others' opinions	NOT ASKED
12. Importance of 10 different sources of information on the Treaty	NOT ASKED
13. Who specifically would like to hear from (re: previous Q)	NOT ASKED
14. Would not ratifying the Treaty be a good or bad thing?	12. Same, except added "for BC" at end
15. Biggest risk in not ratifying	13. Same

	14. Free vote in legislature a good idea or bad
	15. If "Good idea" on Q14, reasons you say that
	16. If "Bad idea" on Q14, reasons you say that
	17. How would feel about a free vote on the Treaty in legislature if own MLA used four different means of gathering input from constituents, respectively
	18. How important that own MLA consider six different "information sources and other considerations" in deciding how to vote on Nisga'a Treaty, respectively
16. Biggest benefit of ratifying	NOT ASKED
17. Support or oppose the Treaty	31. Same, except "and based on everything we've talked about in this survey" is added early in the Q
	32. If "Don't Know" to Q31, which way currently leaning
18. How likely change mind to become supportive over next few months	33. Same
19. How likely change mind to oppose over next few months	34. Same
20. Should the Treaty be put to a referendum	19. Very similar phraseology as in Aug. 98 for half the sample, but other half was asked a question tapping same issue with different phraseology
	20. If "Yes" to Q19, main reason you feel this way
	21. If "No" to Q19, main reason you feel this way
21. If "Yes" to Q20, if no referendum on Treaty, how affect your support/opposition	22. Same
	23. Would free vote in legislature be good substitute for referendum on the Treaty
	24. Statements concerning a referendum on Treaty: a) Hardly worth spending up to $10 million on a referendum when total amount BC will pay under the Treaty is $65 million b) Referendum will only divide the province and create more conflict c) Referendum where majority gets to decide on minority rights is just not right or fair d) Referendum will do nothing to resolve the issue … e) Nisga'a people are voting on the treaty in a referendum; it's only fair that the rest of BC gets a chance to do the same f) We need to resolve land claims now; a referendum will never resolve anything, just like in Quebec g) Some BC politicians say the treaty should be ratified in a referendum of all Canadians; I'm opposed to the idea that the 26 million Canadians outside BC, who outnumber us, would determine what happens on this BC issue

	h) The Nisga'a Treaty amends the Canadian Constitution and, by BC provincial law, the Treaty must be subject to a province-wide referendum i) Even if the Nisga'a Treaty doesn't change the wording of the Constitution, it's a big enough change to the way Canada and BC are governed that we must have a referendum
	25. Which more important to you: having your say on the Treaty in a referendum, or that the Treaty is ratified so BC can get on with resolving land claims
	26. Statements about the Nisga'a Treaty and treaty negotiations more generally: degree of agreement or disagreement a) I'm concerned that signing treaties with aboriginal peoples will create 50 or more separate Indian states in BC b) I don't think the Nisga'a people will spend the money they receive wisely, and I expect they'll come back to ask for more c) I'm opposed to the Treaty because it is too racist, since only Nisga'a people can vote for members of the Nisga'a government d) The Nisga'a Treaty creates a Nisga'a government that is as powerful as a province, and that's wrong e) Negotiating and signing treaties with aboriginal peoples gives them a special status that no other group in the province has, and that's unacceptable
	27. Follow-up to respective statements in Q26: Suppose you knew that ... ; would this make you feel better or worse about the Nisga'a treaty (5-point scale) a) The Nisga'a government won't be separate, but instead will be like other municipal governments in BC, subject to all Canadian and BC laws ... b) The amount of the cash settlement agreed upon in the Treaty is final ... [and] paid over a period of 15 years and will be managed by the Nisga'a government for economic development ... not divided up among individual Nisga'a people c) Non-Nisga'a people who choose to live in the Nisga'a territory will be ensured representation on health and education boards; they will be able to appeal any decision that affects them ... d) The Nisga'a government will have the powers they currently have as a band council along with those commonly available to all other BC municipalities e) In signing treaties, BC aboriginal peoples will give up the special status they have under the Indian Act, including not paying taxes, and their lands and citizens will be fully subject to provincial laws in ways that they are not subject to today

	28. Reasonableness of the total $490 mil. value of the Treaty, given everything else you know or have heard about the treaty
	29. If "Unreasonable" to Q28, does each of the following make you any more or less concerned about the amount of money agreed upon in the Treaty: a) BC pays $65 million ... Canadians in other provinces will contribute more than 2 dollars for every dollar British Columbians contribute b) Federal government currently spends almost $1 billion per year in BC in Indian Act payments ... [that] will be phased out as more treaties like Nisga'a Treaty are signed and ratified c) Governments will begin to get some of the money back as the Nisga'a become the first aboriginal group in Canada subject to all provincial and federal taxes d) The uncertainty caused by unresolved land claims is stopping billions of dollars in investment and thousands of new jobs in BC e) Local businesses in the NW believe the Treaty is a good thing for their area because ... f) This treaty will be the first time in decades that we in BC get more cash back from the federal government than we send to Ottawa ... g) Taxpayers will provide millions of dollars to cover the cash settlement under the Treaty, but then the federal and provincial governments will continue to provide funding to help offset the cost of providing public services to the Nisga'a people h) Settling treaties in urban areas means that even more cash will be paid out to aboriginal peoples since there's not likely any land put on the table by the provincial government in those areas i) TO HALF THE SAMPLE ONLY: The amount of the cash settlement agreed upon in the Treaty is final at about $56,000 per Nisga'a; it will be paid out over a period of 15 years TO OTHER HALF OF THE SAMPLE: The cost of the cash settlement agreed upon in the Nisga'a Treaty is final at about $16 per British Columbian, or just over a dollar each year for 15 years; the cash will be paid out over a period of 15 years j) The cash settlement in the Treaty will not be divided among individual Nisga'a people, but will be managed by the Nisga'a government
	30. Which statement comes closer to your view: a) As the only province without treaties, it's time for BC to resolve land claims ... Nisga'a Treaty will help end economic uncertainty that's costing us investment and jobs ... and begin making dependent aboriginal communities more self-reliant

	i) TO HALF THE SAMPLE ONLY: ...The Nisga'a Treaty is the result of decades of negotiation and compromise, and we should therefore ratify it now ii) TO OTHER HALF OF THE SAMPLE: ... They say a negotiated settlement like in the Nisga'a Treaty is better than having the courts decide this for us and we should therefore ratify it now b) TO ENTIRE SAMPLE: While it is important to resolve aboriginal land claims, having no treaty is better than having a bad treaty ... Nisga'a Treaty creates a race-based government with special status, costs too much in cash and land, and sets bad precedents ... Instead of ratifying this treaty, they say we can just go back to the table and negotiate a better deal
22. Age	35. Same
23. Formal education	36. Same
24. Union member in household	NOT ASKED
25. Private or public sector union	NOT ASKED
26. Are you an aboriginal person?	37. Same
27. Total household income before taxes	38. Same
0. Sex (determined, but not asked)	0. Same

Appendix 7: Methodology

Data Types and Venues

The British Columbia section of this monograph is based upon archival records, face-to-face interviews conducted with sixteen individuals, and other records procured through Freedom of Information requests. Newspaper reports were used primarily for some contextual and chronological information and the Postscript. The Australian research reported in Chapter Eight involved fourteen interviews, plus records procured through a Freedom of Information request. A few Australian documents (mainly reports of public opinion research conducted for the Council for Aboriginal Reconciliation) were also used. Finally, some Australian newspaper reports were consulted, especially to provide elaboration, contextualization, or time-ordering of events to which interviewees referred.

Interviews on the topic of federal public opinion research surrounding two issues—the Nisga'a Treaty and an apology to Canadian aboriginal people—were conducted with Canadian federal officials and their pollster. These were done primarily in July and September of 1999. Interviews with Australian federal officials and their pollsters were conducted in April 2000. As in the Canadian research, most interviews were tape-recorded. The Australian interviews included virtually all of the key players, plus some other individuals who were well placed to be knowledgeable about public opinion research on reconciliation and other Indigenous issues.

BC and Australian Polling Interviews and the Relinquishment of Anonymity

Consider first interviewing conducted in British Columbia on the topic of polling. In early 2000, five "primary" interviews were conducted with persons who were elected or appointed officials or contractors in the British Columbia government during the autumn of 1998. A sixth primary interview was conducted at that time with the pollster on the Nisga'a project. A supplemental seventh interview of 90 minutes was conducted in early 2004 with a former member of the NDP caucus in the legislative assembly. Primary interviewees were selected by means of a snowball sampling procedure. Those interviews ranged in length from 75 minutes to 2 hours and 40 minutes. Most were about 2 hours, as was the average. Parts or all of most interviews were tape-recorded.

These interviewees were guaranteed anonymity at the time of the interview. When the nature of the research write-up evolved into a monograph focusing in large part on the Nisga'a case study, interviewees were asked if they would relinquish their anonymity, basically, for the sake of clarity of the historical record on a treaty of landmark significance in the unfolding of relations between aboriginal people and the larger Canadian society. Some agreed to relinquish their anonymity, but some did not. Therefore, in order to respect the decisions of the latter, some of the above description of interviewees is deliberately vague and a deliberate mix of styles for referencing interviewees is used throughout the book. Real names are usually cited for those who gave permission. Interviewee identification numbers are sometimes used for those who declined to relinquish anonymity while, at other times, they are simply cited as "one interviewee." To further protect the anonymity of those who requested it and to guard against inadvertent identification by a process of elimination, sometimes those who agreed to relinquish their anonymity are cited by identification number only or merely as "one interviewee." These procedures result in a slight loss of specificity in the historical record provided here, but I consider them necessary in order to respect the original terms of the consent agreement signed by interviewees.

Similar principles were applied in the referencing of Australian interviewees, some of whom also agreed to relinquish their anonymity for certain quotations. This involved detailed and protracted consultations with two of these Australians, including one interviewee's rephrasing of originally quoted remarks in order to achieve greater clarity or precision.

The BC Advertising Interviews

Eleven persons (including two who had also been interviewed about the polling) were interviewed in conjunction with their involvement in the British Columbia advertising and public information campaign. Those interviews ranged in length from just over 1 hour to just over 3 hours and averaged slightly less than 2 hours (108 minutes). These interviewees were also selected on the basis of a snowball sampling procedure. These interviewees were given a more elaborate consent form that provided options ranging from anonymity to degrees, types (e.g., pseudonym), and timing of disclosure of identity. Only two of the eleven requested anonymity, and only two required that I obtain pre-publication permission from them for any remarks of theirs that I intended to quote with attribution. A very small amount of intended text was eliminated for want of such permission. Only one person from whom I requested an interview refused to be interviewed.

The interviewees included all of the key players and key decision makers in the British Columbia polling, advertising, and public information campaigns. Ministry of Aboriginal Affairs personnel involved in responding to calls from members of the public on the toll-free telephone line were not interviewed.

Documentary Data

Archival data was also accessed, in the form of questionnaires and polling reports lodged with the British Columbia Archives. Copies of most of the advertisements used in the campaign were also obtained. Freedom of Information requests to the British Columbia government yielded valuable data, such as advertising requisitions and contracts, media synopsis reports, and some ads. For the Australian case study, various documents, such as the focus group and survey reports, were obtained from electronic archives available on the Web.

Reliability and Validity

Memory decay has to be a concern vis-à-vis the reliability and validity of the British Columbia data. Most of the polling-related interviews in British Columbia were conducted approximately fifteen to eighteen months after the events in question, while most of the advertising-related interviews were conducted almost six years after the events. All of the interviewees had moved on to other responsibilities and preoccupations. However, by virtue of the fact that many of the same questions were posed to different interviewees, some cross-validation was achieved. Sometimes documents shown to interviewees proved to be a productive prod to their memory. A validity check of a sort was also obtained through the supplemental interview with a person who was not part of the inner circle and therefore was able to offer a more detached perspective.

Australian interviews were conducted within four months of some of the key events and in the midst of other key events. Hence, political sensitivity, rather than memory decay, was the main issue. Yet, as an outsider from so far away, I probably received some sensitive information that would not have been shared with an Australian researcher. Close consultation with two Australian interviewees was conducted from September through December 2005 for purposes of fact checking and to ensure that ethical obligations to interviewees were honoured in both letter and spirit. A negligible amount of information was deleted due to these consultations with Australians, and most of it was replaced with newspaper accounts. In the Australia chapter and throughout the book, where interviewees are named and quotations are attributed to identifiable interviewees, it is with their permission.

Also of relevance to the issue of the validity of the data are possible errors of omission or fallacious assumptions by the researcher. To combat such possibilities, interviewees were asked, "What am I overlooking or in what ways am I off the mark in trying to understand how public opinion was processed on the Nisga'a / reconciliation issue?" A corresponding question was asked about the advertising campaign for those who were interviewed about it. Interviewees endorsed my approach and, at other points in the interview, corrected me when my questions seemed to distort the reality that they had experienced.

It is important to bear in mind that individuals whose career is in communications often speak with a dramatic flair that must be discounted somewhat. Thus, notwithstanding the temptation of uncritically accepting a colourful quotation, I had to be diligent in carrying out a researcher's normal obligations of cross-validation.

Unquestionably, some British Columbia interviewees did engage in what I considered to be calculated lying, a fact that did not surprise some interviewees when I mentioned that it was happening. At times, though, there was a subtlety to the lying. For instance, one interviewee who lied to me also referred me to another person who, I concluded from subsequent efforts at cross-validation, gave me a truthful account of the same events. I came to realize that even almost six years after the Nisga'a campaign, some participants in it genuinely feared repercussions. Furthermore, the identifiable instances of lying involved an infinitesimally small proportion of the interview data collected. Most interviewees were very generous with their time, and many went to great lengths to be helpful and accommodating, at the cost of significant inconvenience to themselves.

In important respects, politics has become the art of impression management. Much advertising, of course, is impression management developed to an art form. The combination of the two in political advertising (product and process) makes for particular challenges of reconstructing realities when a researcher comes along years after the events being studied and is dealing with people for whom impression management is the basis of their livelihood. These challenges are of particular relevance to sociologists' interests in networks of power and influence. For instance, it is in some individuals' interests to let others think that they are particularly close to the Premier when, in fact, they might have access but that access is not extraordinary. When political regimes change, it is also in some people's best interests to minimize notions of how much influence or access to power they had in the former regime. Furthermore, in any political capital, and perhaps especially in relatively small capitals such as Victoria and Canberra, players in the game of politics are prone to engage in speculation, make assumptions, and feed rumour mills. All of that can contribute to the creation of certain putative "facts" that actually bear little relation to the reality lived by those who are subject to the speculation, assumptions, and rumours. Thus, a large part of the interviewing done for this project involved seeking multiple individuals' recollections of particular phenomena or working relationships. That was true in all the research venues.

Ethics and the Ottawa Component of the Research

Finally, I wish to comment on ethics and this book's paucity of references to the Ottawa component of the research project. The project was approved at the outset by the research ethics committee at The University of Calgary. When the research moved into the advertising campaign in British Columbia, that part of the project also received formal ethics approval. In addition, my final report to the research ethics committee on this project received formal approval. That report explained the situation below.

An article-length manuscript based on the research into the Canadian federal government's handling of the Nisga'a Treaty and an apology to aboriginal people was submitted to a Canadian academic journal. Only one of the journal's anonymous referees submitted an assessment. That assessment contained the unsubstantiated and unelaborated accusation that my write-up treated respondents unethically. The allegation was shocking to me for various reasons, including the fact that two of the key interviewees for that research had vetted parts or all of the manuscript and were quite complimentary about it. The journal editor acceded to my request to obtain substantiation of the referee's serious allegation, but the referee refused to co-operate despite three requests from the editor. The incident has left me totally perplexed. I have asked myself whether I have an ethical blind spot. I have also wondered whether I might be a naïve victim of academic politics played by the referee. I am also cognizant of an ethical obligation to publish the findings of my Canadian federal government research, in light of the investment of time by the interviewees in that part of the project.

The Ottawa findings have been incorporated into this book, in that they are an important part of what went into many of the propositions contained in Chapter Nine. I doubt that they will ever be the primary focus of another publication effort on my part, but that remains to be seen.

Appendix 8: Interview Guide for Polling Interviews

Note: The following was developed for data collection in the Government of Canada. It was revised in the field, as appropriate, for the Government of British Columbia's handling of the Nisga'a Treaty. Some questions were deleted. Other questions were added, such as those dealing with the atypicality of the Nisga'a Treaty polling, the role of the Premier and other particular individuals in the polling, the conduct of briefing meetings, and the use of the polling data.

I. CONCERNING PUBLIC OPINION POLLING IN GENERAL

1. a) Is it difficult to get the authorization or resources to do polling on aboriginal issues?
   b) How big is the department's budget for polling? Under what label is that budget found in the annual Estimates tabled in Parliament?
   c) Does the department do a periodic poll at regular intervals? How often does it commission public opinion polling of its own or participate in omnibus surveys?
   d) Does the department subscribe to a polling service (e.g., Decima Quarterly Report)?
   e) To what extent is there competition among government departments (e.g., DIAND, PCO, Canadian Heritage) regarding polling on Native issues? Who are the main competitors, and what form does that competition take?
   f) What organizational resources (e.g., FTEs, organizational units) are devoted to analysing and other processing of poll data?

2. a) Typically, through what steps does a request to do such polling go? What are the decision points?
   b) Whose approval is most crucial?
   c) Apart from budgetary considerations, what kinds of factors might prevent a proposed poll from being conducted?

II. CONCERNING POLLING ON THE NISGA'A TREATY

3. a) What public opinion data were available?
   b) When? / How often?
   c) In what form? (many Qs v. few? BC sample only?)
   d) From whom (Firm)?
   e) Commissioned by whom?
   f) Whose idea was it originally to do the polling?

4. a) Role of your organization in formulating the questionnaire?
   b) Any disputes in question phraseology or translation?
   c) Any disputes regarding sampling?

5. What is the path of the data through the organization?

6. Gatekeepers of the data—e.g., who selects what results will be passed upwards to the senior-most levels of the department?

7. Others with whom you met about the results (inside & outside your department)?

8. a) What interpretations were placed upon the data?
   b) By whom?

c) Challenged or reinforced by whom?
d) Any negotiations on the meaning or importance of the findings?
e) What happens to ambiguity, contradiction, and caveat as results are passed up the hierarchy? (How are they transformed or eliminated?) Can you give me an example?

9. a) Role of previous encounters with public opinion data in shaping how these data were processed?
    b) In general, how much institutional collective memory for other public opinion data is there? (Institutional memory providing comparisons?)

10. a) On the Nisga'a matter, were there any leaks of data to outsiders?
    b) Typically, what happens when a leak of public opinion data occurs?

11. Was any use made of the Nisga'a data by others? Polling "wars"?

12. a) What selection criteria were used in reporting public opinion polling data to the Minister?
    b) What agenda would be served by those selection criteria?

13. a) Typically, what level of statistical analysis (simple frequencies v. scaling v. sector analysis v. multiple regression analysis of causation, etc.) is used on the public opinion data that you come across in this department?
    b) Was that the case with the Nisga'a Treaty data?

14. How much influence did the public opinion data on the Nisga'a matter have in shaping the policy of the government?

III. CONCLUSION

15. How has the existence of Access to Information legislation affected the way in which public opinion polling is handled in the government?

16. Can you give me any examples of important types of public opinion questions that never get asked, that you can think of?

17. What am I overlooking or in what ways am I off the mark?

Appendix 9: Interview Guide for Advertising Interviews

Note: Not all questions were asked of all interviewees. As the need for clarification or cross-validation arose, some interviewees were asked questions not shown here. They dealt mainly with historical particularities, chronology, the involvement of the Premier, partisanship, and interpersonal relations on the team.

1. a) What was your position at the time of the Nisga'a advertising campaign?
    b) With which firm/organization?
    c) I'd be interested in knowing a bit about your own career and educational background.

2. a) What was your role in the campaign?
    b) Did you attend focus group meetings? How many? With whom? Receive reports?
    c) Inside your agency/unit, who were the key players on this campaign?

3. a) With whom in government did you work? (D. McArthur, J. Heaney, I. Reid, J. Ebbels, Other?)
    b) How often did you communicate with McArthur? Heaney? Reid? Ebbels? Other?
    c) Did you ever meet with Premier Clark on the Nisga'a campaign file?

4. Did you work with Daniel Savas, the pollster, at all?

5. a) Have you ever read any of Dick Morris's book, *Behind the Oval Office*?
    b) Was it recommended to you for the Nisga'a campaign?
    c) What was the role of that book in the Nisga'a campaign?
    d) Was there any explicit talk about using what Morris calls a strategy of "triangulation"?

6. a) Who was in control of the Nisga'a campaign?
    b) Who vetted the ads?
    c) Who was in on the decision making about what would run and what would not?

7. a) What agencies got work on the Nisga'a campaign? Which ones got the lion's share?
    b) Was there any division of labour among the agencies?
    c) How was competition between agencies manifested? How did that affect the campaign?

8. a) What was the overall strategy of the Nisga'a campaign? What were the main elements of the strategy?
    b) What were the dates of the campaign(s)?
    c) What was the extent of the campaign:
        i)   media used
        ii)   geographically
        iii) frequency
        iv)   duration (e.g., number of weeks)
        v)   length of ads (e.g., 30 seconds; half page v. full page)
    d) What were your overall instructions? (e.g., "Money is no obstacle"; "Give us a Coca-Cola or a McDonald's type of campaign"; "Go well outside the mainstream of political ads"?)

172 · THE NISGA'A TREATY

e) In what ways did the campaign show Glen Clark's imprint? (e.g., How different was its substance from what it would have been if Mike Harcourt had ordered it?)

f) NOT ASKED: How was the overall ad *content* strategy developed (e.g., whether to use celebrities, whether to use emotional appeals, whether to be aggressive v. educational)?

g) To what values was the campaign pitching? (Was it seeking to tap into some perceived new consensus in BC?)

h) What metaphors were guiding the strategy of the campaign (e.g., military v. chess v. commerce v. medical v. sports)?

i) What were the main differences between the Nisga'a campaign and, say, a McDonald's campaign?

j) Emotionally, did this campaign feel different than other progressive campaigns you've run? If so, how?

k) How, and how extensively, and where were the ads tested?

9. a) Did you or any other advertising personnel have any input to the construction of the polling questionnaires?

b) How did the advertising campaign use polling data?

c) Did you see the actual poll data? If so, in what level of detail? Did you ask for specific cross-tabulation computer runs?

10. a) You might want to bring out an actual ad to help you in answering this next question. Can you describe for me an important specific instance where polling data had an effect on an ad? What were the conversations like?

b) Can you give me some additional specific examples of how an ad was changed or dropped or re-targeted as a result of polling results?

c) How would you describe the overall impact of polling on the ad campaign?

d) How would you describe the overall impact of the ad campaign on the polling?

11. a) What were the biggest challenges in the campaign?

b) Main frustrations?

c) Main professional or creative satisfactions?

d) Main political satisfactions?

e) Most difficult decisions?

f) Biggest mistakes?

12. a) When did the ad campaign begin? End?

b) When did Tony Penikett replace Doug McArthur?

c) When was the "rapid response" team disbanded?

d) Were there tight time constraints (e.g., in making the TV ads or the *A New Journey* video)? If so, how did that affect the campaign?

13. Was there much disagreement on:

a) geographical placement?

b) timing?

c) frequency?

d) placement (programs, e.g., *Hockey Night in Canada*)?

14. a) With such a big project, I imagine that some egos got inflated, and other egos got deflated. Can you give me a sense of that? (NOT ASKED: Follow-up question about the micropolitics of inclusion and exclusion regarding access [who gets invited to meetings and who does not].)

b) Around what issues did conflict and tension emerge? Who was in each camp?

15. Tell me about the disagreement over using Glen Clark himself in an ad.

16. Were there any crises that emerged in the Nisga'a campaign?

17. a) Did the opponents of the Treaty run a concerted ad campaign of their own? If so, how would you describe it? Cost; duration; frequency; strategy; content.

    b) Tell me, please, about the to-ing and fro-ing of those two campaigns with each other. For instance, did you seek to rebut their ads directly? Other?

18. What am I missing, or in what way am I off base in trying to understand the important things about the dynamics of this ad campaign and what was driving it and how it related to the public opinion polling and focus groups?

19. Is there anything else that you'd like to mention?

Thank you very much!

Appendix 10: Substantive Topics in Australian Telephone Survey, January 28-February 14, 2000

A1. Importance of Aboriginal issues relative to other issues

A2. Perception of Aboriginal people as disadvantaged or not

A3. Comparison of Aboriginal living conditions with those of other Australians

A4. View on
   a) Aboriginal people treated harshly and unfairly in past
   b) Formal acknowledgement that Australia was occupied without Aboriginal consent
   c) Formal acknowledgement of Aboriginal people as original owners of traditional lands and waters

A5. Probe reason why disagree with question A4c

A6. View on
   a) Equal rights for all Australians
   b) Recognition of Aboriginals' traditional beliefs and cultures
   c) Contemporary Aboriginal disadvantage due to past treatment
   d) Governments apologizing on behalf of the community
   e) Need for government programs to reduce Aboriginal disadvantage
   f) Stop talking about past treatment of Aborigines and get on with the future
   g) Today's governments should not have to apologise because Australians today were not responsible for what happened to Aborigines in the past
   h) Too much special government assistance for Aboriginals
   i) Efficacy of government expenditures on Aboriginals
   j) Aboriginals not doing enough to help themselves
   k) Adequacy of government help to Aboriginals
   l) The nation should be trying to help Aboriginals become more financially independent and self-reliant

A7. Appropriateness of government apology: Which comes closer to your view: A6d *or* A6g?

A8. Locus of responsibility: Which comes closer to your view: A6c *or* Aboriginal people have mainly themselves to blame for their current disadvantage?

A9. Special rights: Aboriginal entitlement to

A10. Importance of the reconciliation process

A11. In principle, would a document of reconciliation help relations between Aboriginal people and the wider community?

A12. Preference for the nature of a document of reconciliation: Legally enforceable through treaty or statute *or* merely guidance

Appendix 11: The Australian "Draft Document for Reconciliation" (Section A)

(issued June 3, 1999)

Speaking with one voice, we the people of Australia, of many origins as we are, make a commitment to go on together recognizing the gift of one another's presence.

We value the unique status of Aboriginal and Torres Strait Islander peoples as the original owners and custodians of traditional lands and waters.

We respect and recognise continuing customary laws, beliefs and traditions.

And through the land and its first peoples, we may taste this spirituality and rejoice in its grandeur.

We acknowledge this land was colonised without the consent of the original inhabitants.

Our nation must have the courage to own the truth, to heal the wounds of its past so that we can move on together at peace with ourselves.

And so we take this step: as one part of the nation expresses its sorrow and profoundly regrets the injustices of the past, so the other part accepts the apology and forgives.

Our new journey then begins. We must learn our shared history, walk together and grow together to enrich our understanding.

We desire a future where all Australians enjoy equal rights and share opportunities and responsibilities according to their aspirations.

And so, we pledge ourselves to stop injustice, address disadvantage and respect the right of Aboriginal and Torres Strait Islander peoples to determine their own destinies.

Therefore, we stand proud as a united Australia that respects this land of ours, values the Aboriginal and Torres Strait Islander heritage, and provides justice and equity for all.

SOURCE: Council for Aboriginal Reconciliation (1999).

Appendix 12: The Final Australian "Document Toward Reconciliation"

We, the peoples of Australia, of many origins as we are, make a commitment to go on together in a spirit of reconciliation.

We value the unique status of Aboriginal and Torres Strait Islander peoples as the original owners and custodians of lands and waters.

We recognise this land and its waters were settled as colonies without treaty or consent.

Reaffirming the human rights of all Australians, we respect and recognise continuing customary laws, beliefs and traditions.

Through understanding the spiritual relationship between the land and its first peoples, we share our future and live in harmony.

Our nation must have the courage to own the truth, to heal the wounds of its past so that we can move on together at peace with ourselves.

Reconciliation must live in the hearts and minds of all Australians. Many steps have been taken, many steps remain as we learn our shared histories.

As we walk the journey of healing, one part of the nation apologises and expresses its sorrow and sincere regret for the injustices of the past, so the other part accepts the apologies and forgives.

We desire a future where all Australians enjoy their rights, accept their responsibilities, and have the opportunity to achieve their full potential.

And so, we pledge ourselves to stop injustice, overcome disadvantage, and respect that Aboriginal and Torres Strait Islander peoples have the right to self-determination within the life of the nation.

Our hope is for a united Australia that respects this land of ours; values the Aboriginal and Torres Strait Islander heritage; and provides justice and equity for all.

SOURCE: Council for Aboriginal Reconciliation (2000, Appendix 1).

References

Newspaper and Internet

Beatty, Jim

1998a "Victoria to spend $5 million to promote Nisga'a deal." *Vancouver Sun*, October 17, p. A1.

1998b "Nisga'a Interactive Forum hosted by province's public broadcaster." *Vancouver Sun*, November 6, p. B6.

1998c "Ceremony opens Nisga'a Treaty debate: Representatives follow the path of ancestors to Victoria and find the doors open." *Vancouver Sun*, December 1, p. A1.

Bennett, Nelson

2002 "Nisga'a benefits slow to come." *Nanaimo Daily News*, January 14, p. A3.

British Columbia Press Council

1999 "Ted Hayes vs David Black newspapers." *Complaints Report: 1999*. Retrieved April 14, 2004, from <http://www.bcpresscouncil.org/reports/1999.html>.

British Columbia Select Standing Committee on Aboriginal Affairs

1997 *First Report, July 1997*. Retrieved April 14, 2004, from <http://www.legis.gov.bc.ca/cmt/36thParl/cmt01/1997/1report/process.htm>.

Canadian Press

1998 "Nisga'a celebration, advertising costs near $7 million." December 22.

Council for Aboriginal Reconciliation

2000 *Reconciliation: Australia's Challenge—Final report of the Council for Aboriginal Reconciliation to the Prime Minister and the Commonwealth Parliament*. Retrieved October 12, 2005, from <http://www.austlii.edu.au/au/other/IndigLRes/car/2000/16/index.htm>.

Culbert, Lori

1999 "Clark's approval rating at all-time low." *Vancouver Sun*, March 17, p. A1.

Easingwood, Joe

1998 "Editorial edict on Nisga'a could haunt David Black." *Victoria Times-Colonist*, September 27, p. 13.

Elections BC

2003 *Annual Report 2002*. Retrieved November 13, 2003, from <http://www.elections.bc.ca/rpt/2002annualreport.pdf>.

Farrant, Darrin

2000 "PM bar to reconciliation: Wilson." *The Age*, April 18, p. 4.

Grattan, Michelle and Margo Kingston

2000 "The past is the past: Most reject apology to Aborigines." *Sydney Morning Herald*, March 3, p. 1.

Griffin, Kevin

1998 "Editorial order 'abuse of trust': Clark...." *Vancouver Sun*, September 22, p. A4.

Hall, Neal

1998   "Nisga'a land deal taken to court." *Vancouver Sun*, October 17, p. A6.

Hogben, David

1998   "Battle over editorial stance costing money, publisher says...." *Vancouver Sun*, September 25, p. B6.

Howard, Rt. Hon. John

2000   "Reconciliation documents." Press release, May 11. Retrieved August 3, 2005, from <http://www.truncatus.com/wp/john-howard/reconciliation-documents>.

Hunter, Justine and Doug Ward

1996   "Clark loses shine with voters, poll finds." *The Vancouver Sun*, September 18, p. A1.

Indian and Northern Affairs Canada

n.d.   *Nisga* [sic] *Final Agreement in Brief*. Retrieved August 28, 2004, from, <http://www.ainc-inac.gc.ca/pr/agr/nsga/nisgafb_e.html>.

n.d.   *Nisga'a Final Agreement*. Retrieved August 28, 2004, from, <http://www.ainc-inac.gc.ca/pr/agr/nsga/nisdex_e.html>.

n.d.   *Chronology of Events Leading to the Final Agreement with the Nisga'a Tribal Council*. Retrieved August 27, 2004, from <http://www.ainc-inac.gc.ca/pr/agr/nsga/chrono_e.html>.

Kidd, Ros

2000   "Stolen lives." *Brisbane Courier-Mail*, April 4, p. 15.

Kingston, Margo

1997a   "Angry words as Dodson quits Reconciliation Council." *Sydney Morning Herald*, November 5, p. 4.

1997b   "PM threatens election over *Wik* standoff." *Sydney Morning Herald*, November 8, p. 1.

2000a   "Dramatic divide in our race relations." *Sydney Morning Herald*, March 3, p. 2.

2000b   "Well behind and desperate, it's time to reach for the wedge." *Sydney Morning Herald*, April 5, p. 7.

Lavoie, Judith

1998   "B.C. pumped $6.8 million into treaty ads." *Victoria Times-Colonist*, December 23, p. A1.

Leyne, Les

1998   "Orders from on high compromise Black's editors." *Victoria Times-Colonist*, September 22, p. A9.

Link, Rod

2005a   "Nisga'a eye land, oil, gas development." *Terrace Standard*, February 2, p. 1.

2005b   "Editorial: A step forward." *Terrace Standard*, August 24, p. 1

McInnes, Craig

1998   "Pro-treaty ads fail to sway public." *Vancouver Sun*, November 6, p. A1.

2002   "BC First Nations historic rights: Differences still exist, but they can be settled at bargaining table as a result of new policy, Indian leader says." *Vancouver Sun*, November 23, p. B9.

McInnes, Craig and Jim Beatty

1998   "Politicians brawl over Nisga'a Treaty: Provincial party leaders debate on TV after a Native ceremony in Victoria." *Vancouver Sun*, December 1, p. A1.

Nagel, Jeff

2004   "Managing Nisga'a Treaty money a delicate balancing act." *Terrace Standard*, November 24, p. 1.

2005   "New mining town owner meets his neighbours." *Terrace Standard*, February 16, p. 1.

Newspoll Market Research

2000   *Quantitative Research into Issues Relating to a Document of Reconciliation: Summary of Findings.* Canberra: Council for Aboriginal Reconciliation. Retrieved July 22, 2005, from <http://beta.austlii.edu.au/au/other/IndigLRes/car/2000/3/quant.pdf>.

Palmer, Vaughan

1998a   "Nisga'a Treaty being fought in the polling trenches." *Vancouver Sun*, October 23, p. A22.

1998b   "NDP wants it all its own way on the Nisga'a Treaty: It scripted the opening day and boxed in the opposition leader." *Vancouver Sun*, December 1, p. A14.

1998c   "$5 million in spin not enough to distract the voters." *Vancouver Sun*, November 21, p. A22.

Persson, Heather

2005   "Terrace's wait pays off." *Prince Albert Daily Herald*, November 26, p. 4.

Plant, Geoff

2003   "Treaty talks are open book [Letter to the editor]." *Delta Optimist*, September 13, p. 10.

Rinehart, Dianne

1998a   "Pollster attacks BC Liberals' stand on Nisga'a deal." *Vancouver Sun*, October 19, p. A1.

1998b   "51 per cent in BC 'generally' favour Nisga'a autonomy." *Vancouver Sun*, October 22, p. A1.

Saulwick, Irving and Denis Muller

2000a   *Research into Issues Related to a Document of Reconciliation.* Canberra: Council for Aboriginal Reconciliation. Retrieved July 22, 2005, from <http://beta.austlii.edu.au/au/other/IndigLRes/car/2000/1/qual.pdf>.

2000b   *Research into Issues Related to a Document of Reconciliation: Report No. 2—Indigenous Qualitative Research.* Canberra: Council for Aboriginal Reconciliation. Retrieved July 22, 2005, from <http://www.austlii.edu.au/au/other/IndigLRes/car/2000/5/research.pdf>.

Seccombe, Mike

2000   "Ridgeway's link to stolen generation." *Sydney Morning Herald*, April 4, p. 4.

Shanahan, Dennis

2000   "No reconciliation by centenary: Howard abandons deadline." *The Australian*, February 28, p. 1.

Sinoski, Kelly

1998   "Surry trustees oppose using Nisga'a material." *Vancouver Sun*, October 23, p. A1.

Steffenhagen, Janet

1998   "Plan for school lessons on Nisga'a pact defended." *Vancouver Sun*, October 17, p. A6.

Stephens, Tony

2000   "Terra nullius of the spirit." *Sydney Morning Herald*, April 4, p. 1.

Terrace Economic Development Authority

2003   *Five Year Strategic Economic Plan*. Terrace Economic Development Authority. Retrieved December 5, 2005, from <http://www.teda.ca/docs/teda_strategic_plan_2003.pdf>.

Todd, Douglas

2004   "'We look after the land': Series: Nisga'a: After the Treaty." *Vancouver Sun*, October 20, p. B2.

Zimmerman, Sarah A.

2005   "Chief of chiefs turns 90." *Terrace Standard*, August 10, p. 1.

Other References

Bachelard, Michael

1997   *The Great Land Grab: What Every Australian Should Know About Wik, Mabo, and the Ten-point Plan*. South Melbourne: Hyland House Publishing.

Blumer, Herbert

1948   "Public opinion and public opinion polling." Paper read at American Sociological Society, Dec. 28–30, 1947 and published in *American Sociological Review*, XIII (5): 542–549, 1948. Reprinted as pp. 195–208 in *Symbolic Interactionism: Perspective and Method*. Englewood Cliffs, NJ: Prentice Hall, 1969.

1956   "Sociological analysis and the 'variable.'" *American Sociological Review*, XXI (6): 683–690. Reprinted as pp. 127–139 in *Symbolic Interactionism: Perspective and Method*. Englewood Cliffs, NJ: Prentice Hall, 1969.

1969   "The methodological position of symbolic interactionism." Pp. 1–60 in *Symbolic Interactionism: Perspective and Method*. Englewood Cliffs, NJ: Prentice Hall.

British Columbia Archives

1996–1998 "Opinion polls and consumer and commercial surveys 1991–ongoing." GR-2964, Box 17, various files.

Campbell, Colin and George Szablowski

1979   *The Super-Bureaucrats: Structure and Behaviour in Central Agencies*. Toronto: Gage.

Converse, Philip E.

1987   "Changing Conceptions of Public Opinion in the Political Process." *Public Opinion Quarterly* 51: S12–S24.

Council for Aboriginal Reconciliation

1999   *Draft Document for Reconciliation: A Draft for discussion by the Australian people*. Canberra. Public relations document, 4 pages.

Department of the Prime Minister and Cabinet

1999   *Invitation to Submit Proposals for Research into Issues Related to a Document of Reconciliation*. Canberra.

Foucault, Michel

1980   *Power/Knowledge: Selected Interviews and Other Writings, 1972–77.* Edited by Colin Gordon. New York: Pantheon.

Fuchs, Deiter and Barbara Pfetsch

1996   *The Observation of Public Opinion by the Government System.* Berlin: Wissenschaftszentrum Berlin fur Sozialforschung, gGmbH. Electronic version available from <http://skylla.wz-berlin.de/pdf/1996/iii96-105.pdf>.

Ginsberg, Benjamin

1982   "Polling and the transformation of public opinion." Paper prepared for delivery to the American Political Science Association.

Heclo, Hugh and Aaron Wildavsky

1974   *The Private Government of Public Money: Community and Policy inside British Politics.* Berkeley: University of California Press.

Heith, Diane J.

1998   "Staffing the White House public opinion apparatus." *Public Opinion Quarterly* 62(2): 165–189.

Herbst, Susan

1998   *Reading Public Opinion: How Political Actors View the Democratic Process.* Chicago and London: University of Chicago Press.

Hill, Carey

2002   "British Columbia." Pp. 178–188 in *Canadian Annual Review of Politics and Public Affairs, 1996,* edited by David Mutimer. Toronto: University of Toronto Press.

2003   "British Columbia." Pp. 164-178 in *Canadian Annual Review of Politics and Public Affairs, 1997,* edited by David Mutimer. Toronto: University of Toronto Press.

Holstein, James A. and Gale Miller, eds.

2003   *Challenges and Choices: Constructionist Perspectives on Social Problems.* Hawthorne, NY: Aldine de Gruyter.

Human Rights & Equal Opportunity Commission (Australia)

1997   *Bringing them Home: The Report of the National Inquiry into the Separation of Aboriginal and Torres Strait Islander Children From Their Families.* Sydney.

Jacobs, Lawrence R. and Robert Y. Shapiro

1995/96 "Presidential manipulation of polls and public opinion: The Nixon administration and the pollsters." *Political Science Quarterly* 110(4): 519–539.

2000   *Politicians Don't Pander: Political Manipulation and the Loss of Democratic Responsiveness.* Chicago and London: University of Chicago Press.

Kidd, Rosalind

1996   *The Way We Civilize: Aboriginal Affairs—The Untold Story.* St Lucia, Queensland: University of Queensland Press.

Lippman, Walter

1925   *The Phantom Public.* New York: Macmillan.

Lochead, Karen

2004 "Whose land is it anyway? The long road to the Nisga'a Treaty." Pp. 367–334 in *The Real Worlds of Canadian Politics*, edited by Robert M. Campbell, Leslie A. Pal, and Michael Howlett. 4th edition. Peterborough, ON: Broadview Press.

Miller, Peter V.

1995 "The Industry of Public Opinion." Pp. 105–131 in *Public Opinion and the Communication of Consent*, edited by Theodore L. Glasser and Charles T. Salmon. New York: The Guilford Press.

Mills, Stephen

1986 *The New Machine Men: Polls and Persuasion in Australian Politics—How the Opinion Poll Became the Vote that Really Counts*. Ringwood, Victoria: Penguin Books Australia.

Molloy, Tom

2000 *The World is Our Witness: The Historic Journey of the Nisga'a into Canada*. Calgary: Fifth House.

Pétry, François and Matthew Mendelsohn

2004 "How policymakers utilize public opinion." Paper presented to the Annual Meetings of the Canadian Political Science Association, Winnipeg, June 3.

Ponting, J. Rick

1988a *Profiles of Public Opinion on Canadian Native Issues: Module 3—Knowledge, Perceptions, and Attitudinal Support*. Research Report #87-03. Calgary: University of Calgary Research Unit for Public Policy Studies.

1988b *Profiles of Public Opinion on Canadian Native Issues: Module 5—Land, Land Claims, and Treaties*. Research Report #88-02. Calgary: University of Calgary Research Unit for Public Policy Studies.

1991 "Internationalization: Perspectives on an emerging direction in aboriginal affairs." *Canadian Ethnic Studies* 22(3): 85–109.

2000a "Public opinion on Canadian aboriginal issues, 1976–98: Persistence, change, and cohort analysis." *Canadian Ethnic Studies* 32(3): 44–75.

2000b "The political processing of public opinion on aboriginal issues: Toward a general model of state opinion polling." Paper presented at the Annual Meetings of The Canadian Sociology and Anthropology Association, Edmonton, Alberta.

Rutherdale, Robert

2002 "British Columbia." Pp. 164–186 in *Canadian Annual Review of Politics and Public Affairs, 1995*, edited by David Leyton-Brown. Toronto: University of Toronto Press.

Rynard, Paul

2000 "Welcome in, but check your rights at the door: The James Bay and Nisga'a agreements in Canada." *Canadian Journal of Political Science* 33(June): 211–243.

Salmon, Charles T. and Theodore L. Glasser

1995 "The Politics of Polling and the Limits of Consent." Pp. 437–458 in *Public Opinion and the Communication of Consent*, edited by Theodore L. Glasser and Charles T. Salmon. New York: The Guilford Press.

Snow, David A., E. Burke Rochford, Jr., Steven K. Worden, and Robert D. Benford

1986 "Frame alignment processes, micromobilization, and movement participation." *American Sociological Review* 51(4): 464–481.

Spector, Malcolm and John I. Kitsuse

1977   *Constructing Social Problems.* Menlo Park, CA: Cummings Publishing.

Singer, Eleanor

1987   "Editor's Introduction." *Public Opinion Quarterly* 51: S1–S3.

Turner, Ralph and Lewis Killian

1987   *Collective Behaviour.* 3rd edition. Englewood Cliffs, NJ: Prentice Hall.

Woolford, Andrew

2005   *Between Justice and Uncertainty: Treaty Making in British Columbia.* Vancouver: UBC Press.

Index